Communication and Learning Revisited

D1558918

Communication and Learning Revisited

MAKING MEANING THROUGH TALK

Douglas Barnes *&* **Frankie Todd**

Boynton/Cook Publishers
HEINEMANN
Portsmouth, NH

Boynton/Cook Publishers, Inc.
A subsidiary of Reed Elsevier Inc.
361 Hanover Street, Portsmouth, NH 03801-3912
Offices and agents throughout the world

Editor: Peter R. Stillman
Production: J. B. Tranchemontagne
Cover design: J. B. Tranchemontagne and Jenny Jensen Greenleaf

Library of Congress Cataloging-in-Publication Data
Barnes, Douglas R.
    Communication and learning revisited : making meaning
through talk / Douglas Barnes
        p. cm.
    Rev. ed. of Communication and learning in small groups. 1977.
    Includes bibliographical references.
    ISBN 0-86709-356-0
    1. Group work in education. 2. Oral communication.
3. Children—Language. 4. Learning. 5. Interaction analysis in
education. I. Todd, Frankie. II. Barnes,
Douglas R. Communication learning in small groups. III. Title.
LB1032.B334 1995
371.3'95—dc20   95-3111
                                                                      CIP

Printed in the United States of America on acid-free paper
99 98 97 96 95 DA 1 2 3 4 5 6 7 8 9

Contents

Preface

It is not often that a research report survives for nearly twenty years in the hands of practitioners. *Communication and Learning in Small Groups* reported an empirical study of school students working in small groups on tasks given to them by their teachers. It included many quotations from what the students said, in order to throw light on what they gained from the discussions and upon the skills that enabled them to work together. That report is out of print, and we have chosen to write this new book, retaining some aspects of the material and analyses but placing them in a new context of explanation and advice that is addressed to teachers rather than to other researchers. We hope that our research will thereby become available to many more teachers.

Communication and Learning in Small Groups narrated a journey from one set of theoretical and methodological assumptions to a group of rather different ones. *Communication and Learning Revisited* tells the story of another, longer and more reflective journey conducted since we originally collected, analyzed, and wrote up our research.

Not only have we changed; so also have schools, students, and teachers. Despite some of the more worrying issues that schools and teachers must now address, we feel that the discussions still have currency. The ways in which school students of this age talk in small groups have not altered, even though the topics they discuss and the circumstances in which they work may have changed greatly. The need for dialogue in schools is all the more pressing in the context of the many wider issues that come into school along with students, teachers, and parents.

Finally, we warmly acknowledge the professionalism and patience of Rosemary Shapley for her help in preparing the typescript and Joan Lister for her assistance throughout the project. We also thank Wendy Foster for preparing the art work.

We have previously acknowledged our debt to the teachers and students of the two schools who gave us access to their classes twenty years ago.

Chapter One

Talking and Learning

It was our own experience as students and teachers that originally persuaded us that small groups of students, working together, can advance their learning in ways not available when a teacher talks to a whole class. It has never been our purpose to present small group work as a panacea, however; for teachers organizing their students' learning it is one option in the repertoire, an option with its own considerable strengths, as we shall show. Quite young students can and will take joint responsibility for the progress of their learning and gain considerably from so doing.

It was this conviction that led us some years ago to set up a study of small group talk in two schools. One of us had already carried out some study of group talk (Barnes 1976), and we wanted to look more systematically at what happens when children in schools are given a task to discuss. Our report on that research was published (Barnes and Todd 1977) exactly as we had sent it to the Social Studies Research Council which had funded our work. Since then it has been read and used by many teachers on both sides of the Atlantic. It has been recommended to teachers by the National Oracy Project in the United Kingdom (UK), by members of the whole language network in the United States (US), and by Project Talk in Ontario, Canada. Nevertheless, we have always been aware that when we first wrote we had not addressed ourselves specifically to teachers, so that the first edition contained details of the research that some teachers might not find very relevant to their concerns.

The present volume sets out to remedy this. We have retained substantial elements of the original materials but have recast them so that teachers' concerns are addressed directly. Our central task

1

has been to speak to teachers and to make explicit what light our research throws on learning in classrooms. Moreover, we have included a chapter of direct advice about how to manage small group work in classrooms. In the final chapter we have supported this advice with a discussion of how meaning is generated in conversation generally, and how it is generated particularly in discussions directed towards learning. Since the first edition much has been published which has led us to reconsider and clarify what we wrote before.

In this new edition we quote as extensively as before from the tape recordings we made and use the same framework in analyzing them that helped us to understand them in the first place. We have recast our discussion of the progressive construction of understanding during group talk and the part played in this by students' questions, and we also include a chapter (No. 5) which uses our experience during the research to offer advice to teachers who wish to record and study group talk in their own classes or those of colleagues. We hope that teachers will find this useful whether they are informally attempting to understand their students' learning or preparing a thesis for an academic qualification.

Changing Perspectives and Practices

Our interest in children's talking was far from unique, of course. There have for many decades been liberal-minded educators who wished to give students more responsibility for controlling the pace and direction of their learning. Some teachers and theorists in the United States (Anderson 1959; Thelen 1960, for example) had long maintained that small group discussion was an appropriate way of achieving this. What was new in the sixties and seventies was that cheap recording equipment made it possible to investigate in detail what students said, and thus move toward an informed view of what the talk was contributing to their understanding of the topics discussed. English teachers in London (Britton 1969; Martin et al. 1976) transcribed students' talk to show that it contributes to learning. They set out to demonstrate how in discussion students could collaborate to make meanings, could reshape their thoughts and feelings through talk. It became possible also to ask how teachers influenced talk both directly and indirectly, and to explore other ways in which the talk and therefore the learning was influenced by the social context in which it took place. Beyond these were questions about the kinds of talk encouraged or inhibited by these influences and how the value of these kinds of talk as means of learning might be established. It was with concerns such as these that we set out on our research in 1973. We hoped that our work would initiate a tradition of research that would soon move on beyond our thinking. That this has not happened in the way we expected is one of the reasons for this new version of the book.

This is not to undervalue some important initiatives that were taking place in the broad area of language and learning. In the United Kingdom, the Bullock Report (DES 1975) gave an official statement of the importance of group talk in learning, and in 1989 spoken language became for the first time a compulsory part of the UK's National Curriculum for all students. However, in the late eighties this was modified by an official insistence on testing oral skills and on the teaching of Standard English. (There were even ministerial statements which implied disapproval of small group teaching methods.) Nevertheless the British government had funded from 1987 until 1993 a National Oracy Project which took as one of its main tasks to encourage teachers of all subjects to make use of small group talk with students of any age. (*Oracy* was used by Wilkinson et al. 1965 and Wilkinson et al. 1990 to emphasize—in parallel with *literacy*—the importance of spoken language.) The National Oracy Project chose to work through small clusters of schools, organized and partly funded as local projects, and this placed the development work in the hands of thousands of teachers who voluntarily gave up their time to take part.

Both within the project and elsewhere, many UK teachers have enthusiastically adopted group methods and been delighted with the results. The publications of the National Oracy Project, for example, have been filled with articles by teachers in which they quote with delight transcribed extracts from their students' classroom talk. On the other side of the Atlantic, the same has been true of the publications of the Oracy Project in Peel County, Ontario, Canada. Teachers found that students of all ages took part enthusiastically in group talk and that they often displayed unexpected understanding, knowledge, and ability to think for themselves.

In Canada, Brubaker, Payne, and Rickett (1990) published a collection of practical and theoretical articles from different countries which shows how widespread the interest in small group learning had become. In the United States, as a result of the widespread *whole language* movement, many elementary school teachers have become more aware that development in literacy cannot be separated from spoken language and are therefore experimenting with various formats for talk with very young children, including small groups (Short and Pierce 1990; Pierce, Gilles, and Barnes 1993). Two volumes, partly concerned with group talk, were published as the culmination of the Talk Project of Peel County, Ontario (Booth and Thornley-Hall 1991a; 1991b). It appears likely, however, that in North America educators take it for granted that small group talk is for young children and irrelevant to learning in high schools. This is not a view that we share. In Australia, Reid, Forrestal, and Cook (1989) had taken off from the earlier work of Martin and others in London to produce a systematic approach to group work addressed to classroom teachers, which includes a set of categories for recognizing and planning appropriate stages within group learning. This work in Western Australia, like the other projects we have referred to, involved groups of teachers in developing methods of working with groups in their own classrooms.

The spread of small group methods did not take place without the expression of doubts of its efficacy, however. Boydell (1975) and Galton et al. (1980) had reported that most of the talk in groups sitting together in primary classrooms in Britain was not work-related. Bennett and his associates (1984) carried out a general study of the learning tasks given to six- and seven-year-olds, and in the course of it found that younger children sitting in groups spoke to one another primarily (27 percent) to share information and seldom (8 percent) to explain. It seems likely that these depressing results came from classrooms where the students had been given individual tasks and had not received any encouragement to work together or been helped to understand the value of collaborative talk.

In the United Kingdom teachers have not only used small group methods but have undertaken many small-scale studies. Some have been primarily concerned to investigate effective learning from group discussion in subjects such as English literature (Wilson 1976; Dewhirst and Wade 1984), mathematics (Webb 1980), and geography (Baldwin 1976). Others have addressed specific issues: Jones (1988) investigated *inter alia* the effect of students' conceptions of the nature of learning upon their participation in group talk; Phillips (1985) devised a set of functional categories for kinds of talk; and Moss (1989) studied how girls deal with advertising clichés. By the end of the National Oracy Project, some members were investigating oracy more analytically: Des-Fountain and Howe described the kinds of talk that should be valued for learning and Corden identified a range of roles for teachers and the effects of these on group talk (Norman 1992).

At the same time larger scale programs of research into what was called *cooperative learning* were being carried out by teams of researchers in the United States and Israel (Sharan et al. 1984; Yager, Johnson and Johnson 1985; Sharan 1990; Slavin 1990). Galton and Williamson (1992) refer to a survey by Johnson and others (1981) which reported that nearly two-thirds of studies of collaborative methods had reported superior learning from small group work in comparison with standard teacher-class teaching. (Some of the North American work seems to have been limited by an unspoken assumption that the benefits of small group work arise from peer instruction.) Summarizing the outcomes of later work, Sharan (1990, 288) wrote: "The potentially positive effects of cooperative learning on students' achievement have been documented many times in the . . . research literature on cooperative learning." These researchers set up precisely defined versions of "group work" and trained teachers to put them into practice. Sharan et al. (1984) compared class teaching with two ways of working in groups, *Group Investigation*, which emphasized collaborative inquiry and shared responsibility, and STAD (Students Teams and Academic Divisions) which rewarded groups on the basis of the conflated improvement in the test performance of individual members. They were able to show, for example, that collaborative group discussions made possible the most effective academic learning when tested with high-level interpretive questions about literature. This was complemented by the observation that group work is less effective than class teaching when tested by low-level questions requiring merely reproduction of content. Lazarovitz and Karsenty (1990), using pre- and post-tests in the teaching of photosynthesis, concluded that high school students who had worked in groups reached scores superior or equivalent to those who were taught in class and that they gained greater self-esteem and satisfaction in learning.

Conclusions like these have not gone unchallenged and have often been considerably qualified in the course of other studies. For example, Bennett and Cass (1989) warned that groups tended to accept inappropriate explanations in order to maintain consensus and found that there was most interaction in groups that contained one high-attainer with two low-attainers. They also discovered that it was practical tasks that led to more interaction in groups of younger students, but that it was often more open topics (as, for example, talking about stories) that led to what they called *abstract* talk. They also suggested that students need more immediate rewards during the early life of a group, perhaps through short, structured tasks, but that eventually intrinsic motivation is likely to become more important through the influence of group loyalty.

The Israel/United States research tradition has been mainly concerned with testing the outcomes of cooperative learning, paying little or no attention to what goes on in the discussions of a working group. It is possible to read whole collections of papers reporting these researches without seeing a single transcript of students' talk. For this reason their work has not contributed significantly to our understanding of what happens in group discussion and why it is effective for learning. Although their publications propose precise methods for setting up group work (which are discussed in Chapter 4), they do not help teachers decide how they should intervene or what aspects of group talk they should encourage.

In many of the publications there has been a useful stress on the need for teachers to foster and even to teach the skills needed by pupils for successful group work (Kagan 1985). Bennett and Dunne (1992) suggest many exercises that can be used as preliminaries, though they also insist that the learning can be done in the course of substantive tasks. Students need to understand the unspoken ground rules of group work and must be helped to recognize the quality of their own contributions (Biott 1987). Excessive dependence on the teacher's approval has been identified as a major stumbling block, and this is related to fear of failure. Students should be helped to develop *self-evaluating skills* so that they can monitor their own performance. There has been surprisingly little interest in how the norms of teacher-student relationships in a school are likely to influence the students' view of the roles open to them when set into groups, though Galton and Williamson (1992) point out when discussing teachers' instructions to students about group work that "such instructions must be embedded within class norms that encourage cooperation."

Some investigators have set out to define normal stages in the work of a group during a given task (Tann 1981; Reid et al. 1989), a new and useful area of inquiry. Few, however, have considered the place of group work within the range of activities that makes up a lesson or a sequence of lessons (Harlen 1985; Howe 1988). Bennett and Dunne (1992) note in passing how often teachers fail to see to it that there is time for reporting back to the rest of the class, which would provide opportunities for greater explicitness and for the teacher to join in a wider discussion.

Surprisingly there has been little interest shown in the question of whether all kinds of talk are equally useful for learning, beyond some investigation of *high* or *low* cognitive levels. Wells (1989) feared students might be trapped in the everyday thinking they brought from their homes and proposed that teachers encourage what he called *literate thinking*, that is, critical and analytic discussion framed in the explicit terms appropriate to some kinds of writing.

An important change of attitudes and practices has occurred during these years among teachers of foreign languages, who have realized that since their purpose is to enable students to talk and write in real contexts, they are more likely to learn to do so if they have opportunities to use language in ways that simulate these contexts (Widdowson 1978). There is now an extensive specialist literature on communicative approaches to language teaching (Day 1986, for example). Activities recommended for group work include role play, discussion of the subject matter of printed texts, and the collaborative telling and writing of stories. This is an area of the curriculum where group talk has earned an undisputed status.

Thus in 1994 we address our writing to a different situation from that we envisaged nearly twenty years ago. Many books of advice to teachers about how to manage small groups are now available (Howe 1988; Jones 1988; Reid et al. 1989; Galton and Williamson 1992; Bennett and Dunne 1992), as well as two packs of in-service training materials published for the National Oracy Project (Baddeley 1992; Kemeny 1993). We have good reason to know that across the world there are many teachers who are using small group methods in their classes. No longer are we addressing the unconverted alone. However, although teachers are successfully using small group methods which imply a social constructivist view of learning, it seems likely that it is still a minority who could give an account of how the learning takes place or describe the influences that shape students' participation. Although an agenda of practical issues has emerged, no new theoretical framework has been developed on which future research might call, so we have become aware that elements in our 1977 study still have value. In what follows we have aimed to retain those elements of the original work that have not been replaced by subsequent studies while setting them in a new framework that may be more helpful to teachers.

The Purposes of the Study

We take it to be a commonplace that there are relationships between what is known and the social location of the knower. Much of the discussion of these relationships has focused upon large-scale factors such as social class. Education provides a social context set up primarily for the control of knowledge by the patterning of communication. The underlying purpose of this study was to examine the relationship between small-scale aspects of the social interaction of small groups and the cognitive strategies generated in the course of this interaction. We did not wish to test learning outcomes but to carry out concurrent analyses of the social interaction and cognitive strategies as they appeared within the acts of communication themselves.

In planning the study, we made a number of assumptions about thought and its relation to speech. As we maintain later in this chapter, speech functions as a means by which people construct and reconstruct views of the world about them, doing so jointly when the speech is a means of communicating with other people. Thus we set out to investigate the interplay between cognitive and communicative functions of speech in contexts planned for learning.

Our second group of assumptions related to an aspect of this interplay. We assumed that one of the means by which adolescents achieve hypothetico-deductive thinking (formal operations) is through internalizing the viewpoints of other people, and that this internalization takes place in the course of discussion in which different viewpoints are interrelated through talk with others. We hoped to be able to describe those features of discussion through which the participants encouraged or discouraged one another to articulate and interrelate their points of view. We expected that the way in which language was used would be affected by *(a)* the learners and their attitudes to schooling, *(b)* the subject matter and the students' perceptions of it *(c)* the demands laid upon the learners, and *(d)* the social situation in which the learning took place.

Since subject matter must exert an influence on discussion, we chose to work with teachers of several different subjects. In collaboration with them we constructed problem-like tasks which were derived from work that the children were currently doing in class and which we and the teachers judged would be amenable to small group discussion. We originally intended to limit the range of tasks to five types: the interpretation of verbal evidence, written or spoken; the interpretation of apparatus, maps, or pictures; the reorganizing of existing knowledge in order to apply it to a new problem; the planning of methods for testing hypotheses; and the planning of displays of knowledge in a new form. However, these proved not to be well matched with the tasks that the teachers proposed to us, for most tasks overlapped into more than one type.

We wanted to investigate the effects on group talk of three aspects of the situation set up by the teachers: *(a)* the tightness of the task structure, *(b)* the expectations of students on whether or not they would be assessed, and *(c)* the level of familiarity and trust existing between participants in the discussions, including any adults present. This led us toward an interest in the amount and quality of collaboration between the students, their use of hypothetical modes of speech, and the effect of giving them more control over the process of learning. At this later date this last aspect of learning talk in small groups now seems more central than it did then.

We expected to be able to place each example of group talk along a dimension running from intimate to public. We thought that small group talk—in contrast to most talk in conventional lessons—would fall at the intimate end of the scale and that problem-solving in a small group would have characteristics that might be called *exploratory* whenever the speakers thought aloud. These would include: hesitations and changes of direction; tentativeness; assertions and questions in a hypothetical modality that invites modification and surmise; self-monitoring and reflexivity. We expected that exploratory talk would be characteristic of discussions in which students collaborated in restructuring their thinking about a school topic.

A second characteristic that interested us was the level of collaborativeness in a group's approach to a task. We expected this to be shown not only by a cumulative use of one another's thinking but also by attentiveness to the others' social needs and a low level of competition for the right to speak. We expected that handing control over learning strategies to the students would make a wider range of speech roles available to them and enable them to deal with issues and misunderstandings that would not necessarily have been available to a teacher.

Not all of these analyses proved possible. For example, we found that groups achieved and maintained collaboration by many means, not all of them linguistic, so that the markers we had predicted were inadequate to the task of specifying a level of collaborativeness. Similarly with exploratory talk: it was possible to specify surface language features that frequently, (but not always) marked its existence, but it seemed less useful to count these than to trace the patterns by which a group reshaped the content of its thinking as a result of treating one another's assertions as open to modification. However, the idea of reflective thought as a product of collaboration proved to be very rewarding, as will become plain in the following chapters.

The Role of Talk in Learning

It seems important before we illustrate the talk that we recorded to explain why students' talk is an important part of the learning they are engaged in, for it was not only the practical experience of group talk that had caught our interest. Our understanding of what learning is, and how we achieve it, shows the importance of helping learners of any age take an informed and conscious responsibility for how they engage with learning tasks.

Before discussing the contribution of talking to learning it is important to make clear what we mean by *learning*. Nearly all educational psychologists nowadays accept in one form or another the view of learning called *constructivism*: this implies that each of us can only make sense of what goes on around us, and of our part in it, by actively constructing a world for ourselves. Clearly, this is not independent of the other people around us and the way that they understand the world. Nowadays we are very aware of the social element in almost all learning, so that the collaborative element in group talk takes on considerable importance. To understand how talking contributes to learning we have to take into account both what the learner does and the part played in learning by other people. We shall discuss learning from these two perspectives in turn, beginning by considering the learner as an individual and moving to the social perspective in the next section.

Both children and adults continually set up implicit models or pictures of how the world seems to be and use these models both to understand what is happening and to guide their actions upon it. The models thus constructed are far from final but are open to continual modification in the light of new experience, especially when there is evidence that other people see things differently. Sutton (1992, 40), writing about science education, describes it as "learning to see in new ways." People sometimes say, "Ah, I see it differently now," but do not necessarily mean that they have an actual visual image. The models or pictures that students form guide both their interpretation of and their participation in the physical and the social world. To take an example from the physical universe, students' experience in the world outside school leads them to expect that water will become progressively hotter the longer a heat source is applied to it. This will guide their heating of liquid in a science laboratory, but if they record the temperature at regular intervals they will come to a point at which the measurements level off. Of course, in one sense they *know* about boiling, but for many ten-year-olds it will be a revelation to see its effect upon temperature. They will have to reconstruct the model by which they represent the relationship of heating and temperature, and this may take some time and discussion and perhaps further practical demonstration. As this process of *seeing things differently* continues it may well cause changes not only in the student's understanding but in his or her ways of dealing with heat inside and outside school. A similar process takes place in social studies and language arts. In reading the beginning of a story, children may make a premature judgment about a character or event and fail to modify it in the light of later events: they have to learn to be flexible in interpretation. Or an older student may approach events in history with an unspoken expectation that they are shaped primarily by outstanding persons, and this is likely to interfere with the building of the valid network of information and interpretations essential to that subject. It will be seen that the process is less clear-cut in non-scientific subjects, since it is more likely to be concerned with overall preconceptions than with specific conceptual structures. In all these examples, students began with models of how that part of the world operates, but the models had to be modified because of new experience. Such "reconstruction" in the light of new evidence is at the center of learning.

It will be clear from the examples that our most important learning does not take place through the addition of discrete facts to an existing store. Both in understanding the behavior of heat and in learning how to understand a story or historical event, new experience is likely to lead to a reshaping of a wider area of understanding, which may later affect how other similar events are interpreted. These wider changes of understanding do not happen instantaneously; they often need to be worked over. For example, perceptive students may ask themselves or others how far their new picture fits other circumstances. "Does this mean that if I boil fat in a pan it will get hotter than water does?" The new ideas have to find some relationship with the old, for they may challenge and change the pattern of expectations about that kind of phenomenon. One implication of this is that what the learner already knows will lay a central part in the learning. The student's ability to understand the temperature of boiling fat will depend on having at least some understanding of what happens when water boils. Thus it is often important for new learning that existing ideas and explanations are brought to mind and worked upon, and this happens very readily in talk about the topic.

We are proposing a view of learning that places at its center the reinterpretation of experiences that the learner has already had. Through talk the learner can not only reconsider the experience itself but also reshape more generally his or her ideas about such things, ideas previously held in a vague and ill-defined way. Yager, Johnson, and Johnson (1985) call this *cognitive rehearsal*. We are all familiar with the insights that sometimes come when we have long pondered and discussed a problem: it is not caused by new information but by finding a new pattern for what is already known. Moreover, an important part of new learning is testing how far it will go, what other situations and phenomena work in a similar manner. To make the point in terms of the examples, the learner needs to determine the limits and uncertainties that should qualify his or her views about the behavior of heated liquids: Are there any that do not boil, for example? Do outstanding people have no effect upon public events? Is it appropriate to apply everyday ideas about people's motives to understanding political events? Is it inappropriate to judge stories by their verisimilitude? Part of learning is finding how widely applicable newly formed models are for interpreting the cultural and physical world.

The reinterpretation of models of the world in the light of new experience and ideas does not happen instantaneously since the two have to be related in a way that satisfies the learner. In effect, the student must work on his or her understanding. One of the most important ways of working on understanding is through talk, either in formal education or as part of the learning in everyday life. New ways of talking about things lead to new ways of seeing them; talking about a wire as a *conductor* invites the learner to think about something being transported along it (Sutton 1992, 45). However, the pressures of everyday life may not give much opportunity for attending explicitly to events that are puzzling. Neither adults nor children deal eagerly with challenging new ideas, for it is not comfortable to have existing ideas disturbed. Schooling, however, unlike learning in everyday life, is (or should be) designed to give students the opportunity to talk their way with some thoroughness through the dilemmas of learning. It would not be an exaggeration to say that a teacher's central task is to set up situations that encourage students to work on understanding. If schools and colleges do not do this, they are failing their students.

In Chapters 2 and 3 we illustrate how groups of students set about discussing questions set by their teachers. We are able to show that they engage with the tasks set and do so in a rational manner that carries their thinking forward, organizing their progress through the tasks. They also manage their relationships, often with some skill, dealing with disagreement and showing some concern for one another's participation.

In placing stress on the importance of requiring students to work on their understanding, we do not undervalue the teacher's responsibility for presenting new material but this alone is not enough. The importance of talk comes when it provides students with opportunities to relate this new information to their existing understanding of the world. Part of this talk may take place with a tutor, who can guide and redirect thinking, call for greater explicitness, and underline crucial issues. In the next section we show some of the limitations of tutor-led discussion and why it is important for the students also to have the opportunity—indeed, to have the challenge—to work in small groups on the dilemmas that they themselves perceive to be salient.

Learning and the Social Context

We have said that at the center of learning is the procedure by which the learner constructs patterns to explain what has happened, to make links with similar phenomena, and to predict the future—including the likely result of his or her actions. That is what we mean by *understanding* something. The limitation of this way of explaining learning is that it seems to isolate the learner, as if the learning were going on in a social vacuum. Having discussed learning from the point of view of the individual, it is now necessary to consider how the social context affects it.

Human life, including the meanings that give shape to it, is essentially social; most learning is profoundly influenced by that fact. Even when alone we have with us the voices of the society which formed our beliefs and ways of thinking—even our view of ourselves—and formed them so profoundly that for the most part we take them as "how the world is." This has several implications for learning. First, anything done or said is in some sense a contribution to the ongoing dialogues that make up a culture; anything said or written is from one point of view a reply to what has been said or written before. (To write this in 1994 is to echo Bakhtin in 1981, but his work had not been translated and published in Britain when we wrote in 1977. We develop this line of thought in a later chapter.) Second, since students share with family, friends, and teachers their attempts to understand, they do not have to deal with discontinuities alone and unsupported but are profoundly influenced by what other people whom they trust also think. Most teachers are in one sense trusted by their students, but their experience, age, and status are so patently different that at times students gain more from discussion with their peers than with the teacher in class. (A corollary of this is that students bring to school some beliefs and ways of thinking that diverge from what the teacher believes to be true and useful. Since such views are reinforced every day by the experiences shared with family and peers, they can be powerful barriers to new ways of thinking. Every science teacher who has tried to persuade younger pupils that we do not send beams of light from our eyes in order to see will be aware of this.) Third, the pattern of behavior and expectations during class is in general controlled by the teacher, and students who wish to succeed must conform and gain insight into the educational ground rules that are required but not made explicit. That is, classroom procedures imply roles for students which shape how they take part in learning. It is possible that at times these roles constrain students unnecessarily and prevent them from dealing with their more idiosyncratic dilemmas in learning. We deal with this third issue in the remainder of this section.

What distinguishes learning in schools from everyday learning is that in school students have the opportunity to carry out more consciously the processes of constructing understanding and modifying it in the light of additional knowledge and experience. However, the context of such learning is not always very helpful. It is very easy for students to form a misleading impression of what constitutes learning, which will impede their progress, for such misconceptions are all about them.

Lectures and lessons and textbooks often seem to imply that knowledge is made up primarily of information (*facts*) to be memorized, whereas it is understanding and the ability to apply understanding that make for wisdom. Examinations too sometimes seem to tell young people that education is about the memorizing of facts, and television quiz programs reinforce this view. In many lessons the teacher's use of questions to test understanding also seems to imply that all that is needed is to produce the *right* answer. *Right answerism*, as it has been called, misleads some students about what kind of learning is required of them.

An example of this may make this clear. One of us once sat in an English lesson in which the teacher was endeavouring to help a class of thirteen-year-olds think about the meaning of a short story they had just read. To do this she was asking questions about the implications of events in the story, the characters' motives, and the author's purposes. Her intention was to enhance their skills in reading stories; the particular story was almost unimportant. One boy stood up and asked her, "Why don't you write all the questions on the blackboard, and all the answers, and then we can learn them and get full marks?" This boy, and probably other students in that class, had a false understanding of the nature of the learning required of them, and this was likely to lead to a self-defeating strategy. Such misunderstandings can arise even more readily when schooling appears to be the presentation of information by teacher and textbook, followed by testing through oral questions or written tasks. Such students need opportunities and challenges that will enable them to see learning as constructing an understanding, not as reflecting and repeating ready-made formulae whose implications they have not grasped.

Relating new experience to old ways of thinking so that the latter can be modified is at the center of all learning, everyday as well as academic. This can happen in various ways, through well-chosen tasks set by teachers, through practical work, calculations, diagrams, and writing. For some exceptionally self-reliant and well-motivated students, private reading and thinking are enough. But for most students, talk is the most important way of working on understanding. Talk is flexible: in talk they can try out new ways of thinking and reshape an idea in mid-sentence, respond immediately to the hints and doubts of others, and collaborate in shaping meanings they could not hope to reach alone. The support of other members of a group is important, as is the need to reshape one's own ideas to incorporate their diverse ideas. In our research this proved to be an important contribution that members of the groups made to one another's thinking.

Small group talk encourages exploration of ideas, rather than the presentation of certainties. It is useful to make this distinction between talking to explore new ideas because one is uncertain about them and talking in order to present well-shaped ideas in a confident and public manner. Exploratory talk is more likely in a small group of peers partly because the price of failure is lower: even twenty boys and girls can seems a threatening audience when one is uncertain. Members of a small group can risk hesitation and confusion, changes of direction, and rejection of their ideas by the others. The hesitancy and flexibility of exploratory talk is potentially a strength when students are talking in order to reshape and reinterpret ideas.

Traditionally the interactions between teacher and class are intended to help students reshape their understanding, but this talk, important though it is, does not always achieve this. Exploration and reconstruction of ideas through talk is discouraged by the size of the group and by the struggle to get possession of the floor; a brief assertion seems to fit the situation better. Class teaching isolates students by creating competition to respond to questions and the fear of failure (Sharan and Shaulov 1990). It is well known that much teacher-class talk is not so much exploring ideas as testing whether the students can reproduce what the teacher has presented to them (Hoetker and Ahlbrand 1969; Westbury 1972). Students everywhere are asked questions to which the teacher knows the answer, and what is required is not for them to think aloud but to say enough to satisfy the teacher that they have been listening. This leads to long questions and brief replies, often single words; the teacher is responsible for constructing the meanings in the long questions, making little demand on the students to work on understanding. Even when the situation calls for a longer reply, most students will avoid thinking aloud and will endeavour to give a pre-planned answer.

Teacher-led discussion, for all its traditional centrality in class-rooms, too often leads to presentational talk and inhibits explo-ration.

Moreover, teacher-led discussion is often ineffective in identi-fying those dilemmas that need to be dealt with. How can a teacher know what problems each of perhaps thirty young people needs to think through? Tizard and Hughes (1984) have shown that parents, whatever their social background, are far more successful than teachers in engaging young children in talk about the events and concerns of their lives. The discussion led by the teacher has the ad-vantage of the teacher's knowledge and experience and (at best) of the teacher's skill in helping students make their thinking explicit. Yet even the most skillful teacher cannot gain access to students' everyday experiences or focus upon the discontinuities that are im-peding their different trains of thought. This is why small group talk should have a place in every teacher's repertoire of teaching strate-gies, for at best it enables the learners to think through precisely those concerns that each of them needs to clarify.

Some teachers have bravely recorded both the discussion by small groups of a task they have set and at the same time a parallel discussion of the same topic in which they have led the rest of the class. This often proves a salutary experience. It is not easy for teachers to ask the *right question* simply because they do not have easy access to students' previous experiences or to the dilemmas which need to be deal with, while the students cannot usually tell us what they need to reconsider. Sometimes small groups make more progress than the teacher and class simply because they have directed the discussion toward their own needs, even though they could not have explained in the abstract what these were. Learning is a social activity; interaction with peers should not be underrated.

From one point of view, what we are proposing is that students be given more control of their learning and therefore more respon-sibility for how they set about it. Clearly this is not a matter of throwing them in to sink or swim. We have already pointed out that some school-age students have a misleading idea about learning which would impede their progress. There is agreement among re-searchers into small group talk that for success it is essential for the teacher to help students grasp what kind of learning is required. Moreover, giving responsibility to learners does imply that they have accepted the goals of the learning, which is not necessarily the case in schools. Young teachers are often advised to approach group work circumspectly, controlling it carefully by first giving limited tasks and only later handing over to students the responsibility for guiding their work over a period of time. Older students who have accepted the importance of the learning and wish to make progress will need less help in getting underway.

However successful the group discussion, there will be a point at which the teacher should ask the students to make their thinking public in order to help them to achieve greater explicitness and self-awareness in the learning. At this stage, when the students have made progress through the early stages of exploration, the need to present results explicitly and to interact with the teacher's more practiced thinking about the subject will greatly advance learning. (Ways of structuring group work, and its relationship to other patterns of learning during the same courses, are discussed in more detail in Chapter 4.)

If teachers rely too exclusively upon presenting material to students and then testing their grasp of it through questions, they are very likely to underrate the part that the students' own knowledge and ability to make sense of the world can play in learning. In class, students often seem to be much less well provided with knowledge and understanding than they are. We have found that many teachers are amazed when they first listen to recordings of their students talking in groups: they are surprised how much the students understand and even how much relevant experience and information they can bring to the discussion. The explanation is not far to seek. Since teachers control the agenda of lessons, control what count as relevant questions and relevant answers, and control moreover the kind of language in which these can be talked about, the students must master the substantive material of the lesson and at the same time penetrate the teacher's often unspoken preconceptions about how to talk and think about it. It is clearly better to use students' existing knowledge and even more to use their ability to make sense of the world. Treating students as containers to be filled to the brim with facts was already being mocked by Dickens in the last century; we have gone further since we now know how the knowledge and vitality of the *Cissy Jupes* of our time can be put to work for learning.

Of course, information is often essential: we are certainly not wishing to suggest that teachers should not present new ideas and information to their students. Books, demonstrations, video material, and the teacher's own presentations—as well as work with apparatus and visits to observe events outside school—are all essential. But information alone is not enough. Every student needs to relate the new information, new experience, the new way of understanding to his or her existing understanding of the matter in hand. To depend upon the teacher's presentation alone is to expect the learners to arrive without having traveled. When a new experience or idea seems to conflict with our existing way of understanding we can ignore it, and unfortunately we often do just that. But in school students should be helped to face such discontinuities, because they provide the route to new and better understanding.

Making the Recordings

We turn now to our recordings and the choices we made in order to collect them. We wanted to record the talk of thirteen-year-olds; students of this age attend high school in the United Kingdom. We chose this age group partly because we could expect them to manage their intra-group relationships competently and because they could be expected when discussion went well to achieve reflective thought of some complexity. In both these respects the best discussions we recorded far exceeded our expectations. We decided to work with students of average ability rather than highly able boys and girls so that our results could not be discounted as out of the reach of *normal children*. For the first groups whom we recorded we accepted their teachers' judgment of which students were of average ability; for the second set of recordings we utilized a standard test of intelligence to make the selection.

The recordings were made in two high schools situated on the outskirts of a large industrial city; both had a predominantly white, working class intake. William Byrd School drew children from a mixed area of recent community housing and small owner-occupied duplexes. The other, Wickhouse School, was set in an older area of less well-cared-for community housing. As visitors we could certainly sense differences between the students of the two schools. Most obviously, students at William Byrd were relatively accustomed to working in groups but not those at Wickhouse School. We thought that this probably indicated different norms for teacher-student relationships in the two schools.

We decided to work with teachers of a range of subjects, since useful discussion can contribute to learning in any area of the curriculum. However, in the event our choice was determined by those teachers of our groups of students who were eager to work with us, teachers of social studies, English, physics, biology, history, and geography.

When we began we wanted our recordings to be as close as possible to what happens when, at some point in the teaching of a topic, the teacher decides that group discussion would contribute usefully to the students' learning. That is, we wanted the discussion to have a context, to arise from teaching that had gone on before, and to point implicitly to further work after we had left. Thus we chose a school where several teachers were willing now and again to pick up a telephone and tell us that they were planning some work in groups with the pupils we had chosen. We then collaborated with the teacher to devise tasks for the pupils; when the recordings were made each pupil had a "task card" with instructions typed on it. These included the topics to be discussed; sometimes framed in a relatively open manner but often made up of a series of directions for a procedure to be followed or questions to be answered. The tasks sometimes required the study of texts or the manipulation of apparatus. These "tasks" can be found in Appendix A. In Chapter 4 we discuss how the choice and framing of tasks contributes to the success of group talk.

In all social contexts, the patterns of language use provide channels through which membership and status are allocated. That boys and girls experience schooling differently is partly a function of the different language practices into which they have been socialized and of the different valuations that may at one time or another be placed upon these. A similar allocation of status and identity can occur for members of some ethnic groups; however competent their use of language, what they say may be *heard* as less appropriate or less insightful than similar opinions spoken in a standard dialect. During the last twenty years teachers and researchers have become far more aware of the influence of gender and ethnic identity upon children's participation in education. For example, in Israel a large-scale study (Sharan et al. 1984) was centered upon the belief that students from competing ethnic groups should have opportunities for more effective communication and collaboration than the playground allowed, cooperative learning in small groups being used to facilitate changes in attitude and behavior. Both successful *high level* learning and changed attitudes to members of the other ethnic group were recorded, but a test of practical cooperation did not produce positive results.

Several researchers have included gender as one of the variables to be investigated. Bennett and Dunne (1992), for example, reported high levels of on-task talk for both girls and boys in groups of students aged from four to twelve years. They found little abstract talk from either girls or boys in mathematical and technology tasks, but in language arts the girls engaged in more abstract talk (28 percent to 14 percent) than boys. Girls, however, talked less in groups where boys outnumbered them. Tann (1981) found that groups of girls were often consensus-seeking.

In 1973 we did not include issues arising from gender or ethnicity as part of our research into groups, in part because we did not have an analytical framework adequate to explore those interests. Our prior task was to develop a framework for understanding, in general terms, what happens when teachers give students the opportunity to work in this way. We saw to it in one set of the recordings that each group should contain two boys and two girls but it was not possible to obtain gender balance in recordings from our other school. Issues deriving from ethnicity did not arise in either of the schools, since we had chosen them primarily because they would provide us with small group work that was an integral part of teaching in a range of subject areas. However, while our recordings tell us nothing specific about the roles of gender or ethnicity in group work we believe that the discussion that follows is relevant to all students: talk in appropriately designed contexts can help all students to develop new understandings.

Moreover we would now argue that students' discussion has a particularly important role to play in multi-ethnic, multi-lingual classrooms. If talk aids learning (as it does), all students need the opportunity to find their voices in the encouraging context provided by small group work. Furthermore, the rich resources for learning that diversity of experience and perspective bring into the classroom can only be drawn upon if their voices can be heard. This has been argued strongly elsewhere (Department of Education and Science [UK] 1983), as have the problems that may arise from confining classrooms to implicitly monolingual communication as seems to be implied by the UK National Curriculum (Morrison and Sandhu 1993).

In later chapters we explain how we made the recordings and how we analyzed the discussions once they had been transcribed. In what we came to call *the second phase*, we decided to record other groups in the same schools under rather different conditions. We explain what these conditions were and what effect they had upon the talk that took place.

Chapter Two

Collaboration in the Groups

Our first task is to show that thirteen-year-olds can indeed work together and that they can collaborate to clarify their understanding of topics which a teacher asks them to discuss. As set out in Chapter One, we see small group discussion as affording a means for the construction and reconstruction by learners of new views of the world. In other words, engaging in dialogue with others, communicating one's own viewpoint, and considering what others in turn have to say can clarify a learner's existing understandings and help develop new ones.

For this link between communication and learning to be achieved in the course of small group discussion, it is necessary that learners share common purposes and collaborate to joint ends. In this chapter we illustrate and analyze such collaboration in action. We show how groups get started, manage their progress through tasks, and their shifts in topic, utilize different types of contributions to develop new lines of thought, and encourage each other to participate.

In practice, this collaboration is not separate from the joint development of new lines of thinking about the topic in question. However, for the purposes of discussion, it helps to look at collaborative and cognitive aspects separately. Accordingly, we discuss the cognitive strategies which our groups used in Chapter 3.

Taken together, Chapters 2 and 3 demonstrate the high levels of collaboration toward the development of new thinking which these ordinary thirteen-year-olds were able to achieve. In revealing how they went about their work—what the students did to achieve this—the chapters give teachers new to this way of working an idea of what they might expect from their students. Further, the materials provide a number of pointers for the design of small group work in classroom settings which we will explore in Chapter 4.

Tasks, Students, and Recordings

Before going on to discuss our materials we should say a little more about the circumstances in which the groups worked and the approach we have taken to analyzing and commenting on the recordings. As summarized in Chapter One, we recorded an audio tape of students of average ability in two different schools, working on small group discussion tasks which we and their teachers jointly designed and which arose from ongoing classroom teaching. Behind those similarities, there were differences in the way we worked at the two schools in two different phases of the research. In the first phase, when we were attempting to set up a category system to analyze the recordings, we worked at William Byrd School where students were familiar with working in small groups before we came on the scene. We spent a substantial period of time with the same groupings of students. Teachers from different disciplines called us in when they reached a point in their teaching—of geography, or English, or science, for example—when they felt it appropriate to utilize discussion in small groups. Although the teachers varied, the student groups stayed constant and during this first phase of the research these groups became increasingly relaxed about being tape recorded and developed friendly working relationships within the groups and with the researchers (with one exception, as will be seen at the end of this chapter).

Students at William Byrd School had been given an introduction to our research by their teachers before we went in to the school; subsequently, on the first occasion of recording them we explained the aims of our research and what we would be asking them to do. As a further preliminary we recorded some of this conversation (including the teacher's voice), played it back, and then discussed with the students their reactions to hearing this public playing back of their recorded voices. On later occasions we always made time for some sociable chat before asking the students to start the task. We then read out the task card (each student had a copy), asked them to discuss it, switched on the tape recorder, and left the room. The students were asked to switch the recorder off and call us back into the room when they felt they had finished their discussion. These small groups worked in a small side room—to enhance the quality of the recording, they were withdrawn from the classroom to work for us—so they had considerable control over the recording situation. They could—and did—switch off the tape recorder if they wanted to say something not for our ears (they did this less and less as time went by), and they could also play back sections of their discussion so far. After the students called the researcher back in, we always listened with them to a substantial section from their discussion, and the sessions usually ended with jokes and laughter coupled with some serious evaluative comments about the work they had just done. All of this seemed to make the experience something that was shared between ourselves and the students, something that was rewarding to them as well as to us.

During this period we were making approaches to other schools, trying to find a suitable one to cooperate with us. This search took some time so the recording of Groups 5–8 at Wickhouse School came some months after we had started working in William Byrd School. We did not visit Wickhouse School as frequently or get to know the students as well as we came to know Groups 1–4 at William Byrd School. The recordings made at these two schools in the first phase of data collection provided tapes of twenty nine discussions on nine topics (lasting seven and a quarter hours in all) conducted by thirty-two students. In this first phase of the research the students worked in groups of four, each made up of two boys and two girls each.

In the second phase of the data collection at William Byrd School, the conditions the students worked in were rather different. The original plan for our research provided for a quasi-experimental design in phase two in which we hoped to test the effects of task structure and assessment on the communication with the groups. Students from the first year were selected on the basis of their individual IQ scores (whereas in phase one teachers had identified for us a whole class of *average* ability students within the school's banding system). The students who fell within the range we set in phase two came from a number of different classes across the year group. The only way we could record them working together without causing great disruption to a number of teachers was to get all the recording done over a two day period. The students were withdrawn from their—different—classes, allotted to one of eight groups of three boys or three girls, and then asked to work on two different tasks (designed either to have a tight series of focused questions, or to have an open structure) in two different conditions (either expecting that their work would be assessed by their teacher, or told that their discussion was private to them and would not be heard by a teacher). The students did not receive a general introduction to the project from their teacher; they were working in these groupings for this one and time only; they were being recorded on just this one occasion; they didn't have time to get to know us as researchers; and they didn't always know each other well because they came from different classes. This second set of recordings provided sixteen further discussions on two different topics (*Spaceman* and *Gang Violence*) lasting thirty-three and a quarter hours in all.

We subsequently realized that the differences between the recordings in phase one and phase two were far greater than the differences between groups in phase two working under the two different conditions we had set up. The reader will not be surprised by this. Some groups in phase two (Groups 9–16) transcended these difficulties and went on to do some useful work; others were too nervous to fully engage in the tasks. This distinction becomes relevant in later parts of this chapter and in Chapter 3 when we discuss extracts from the students' talk.

Finally, a note on our commentary. Where we quote extracts from group discussions we commonly give interpretive comments, either parallel to or below the extracts. We offer these in the spirit of an introductory guide to terrain that became familiar to us (through our many listenings to the tapes and our analysis of transcripts) but which is new to our readers. Readers' own interpretations, which may well differ from ours, are equally valid. We suggest the reader might first read an extract alone and then reread it with our commentary. All the tasks which we and teachers devised for the students to discuss are given in Appendix A.

Getting Started

We begin by looking at how one of our groups (Group 4 at William Byrd School) starts to discuss the topic set to them. They had been asked to discuss how a national park in the Lake District might set out to reconcile demands for providing facilities for outdoor pursuits and tourism with the need to preserve the natural landscape and protect farming.

1. Alan: Do you think this is a good idea for big National Parks?

Initiates discussion of the usefulness of National Parks, an issue not set on the task card.

I think it is a, an excellent idea because, erm, people like us have the, erm, countryside around us, but other people in the, erm, center of Leeds are less fortunate and do not have, erm, center—countryside that

Answers his own questions and sets up a context for the ensuing discussions of the set questions. (N.B. The school attended by these students is amid fields on the outskirts of the city.)

they can go out into within easy reach.

2. Bill: Yes.	Provides encouragement.
3. Alan: Without being polluted and, erm, chimney stacks all over the place.	Makes the antithesis more explicit.
4. Pauline: This is all right as long as there aren't going to be too many buildings around the place, because it's going to spoil it completely I think. It's all right for a few like cafes or, er, camping sites, a few camping sites. That's all right but nothing else.	Qualifies Alan's contributions, thus turning the discussion towards the set questions. She reinforces part of what Alan said, but suggests that limits need to be drawn.
5. Alan: I think this is one of the best ideas of the, erm, National Parks because they, erm, do not, don't allow buildings to be built without permissions and planning special, you know, so it blends with the countryside and not stuck out like a sore thumb.	Accepts the qualification which leads to his extending the concept of national parks to include the regulation of building.
6. Jeanette: Yes, but it just depends on what the ground's like doesn't it?	Qualifies that part of Alan's statement that refers to blending with the countryside.

We put this passage forward to illustrate how a group can, under some circumstances, collaborate from the start on the coherent and rational construction of understanding. In this case the ideas are likely to be readily available from everyday life, though the topic had previously been discussed in a lesson. There is no sense of the regurgitation of inert knowledge, however, or of the retracing of a familiar path; the students are rearranging their knowledge as they talk and trying out new combinations and implications.

Keeping Going

The next example is from a group that is already some way into its work. In contrast to the extract above, the topic discussed in the next example is scientific. The group (Group 1, also at William Byrd School) had been given these definitions:

> We use the idea of WORK as a measure of how much ENERGY changes from one form to another. WORK is done when a force moves.

The pupils were required to apply these definitions to three given examples and then to think of other examples of energy changes, in order to answer the question: "Is work always done when energy changes form?"

In this case too the group had had preliminary discussion of the topic in class. In answering the question, however, they had to utilise both ideas from everyday life and the given definitions of work and energy. The following exchange occurred when, after some minutes of discussion, the group had dealt with the three given examples.

48. Marianne: Is, is there any things that we don't use energy in?

   Marianne seeks an example to test an earlier assertion by Barbara.

49. David: Yes.

50. Marianne: What?

51. David: Erm, one of these, one of these pylons, holding up a roof, they aren't using energy.

   Puts forward a relevant example.

52. Jonathan: It's constant energy, because if that wasn't there the roof'd fall.

   Jonathan does not use the given test for the change of energy from one form to another but appears to be using a concept equivalent to *potential energy.*

53. David: No, it isn't moving is it? So it can't be using any energy.

   David, using the definition of *work,* challenges Jonathan's assertion.

54. Jonathan: Well it had to use energy in the first place to be put up though.

   Changes his statement to a form which acknowledges the validity of the test.

55. Marianne: Well it's using work.

   Not (apparently) using the given definition of *work.*

56. David: Oh to be put up yes, but when it's there now, it just holds the roof up. It isn't moving; it doesn't have energy.

   David summarizes, relating to one another the two versions of energy previously put forward; he lacks a term such as *potential energy* for labelling one of them.

57. Jonathan: There's a force, as well though.	Checking their agreement on the distinction between *force* and *energy*.
58. David: I know there'll be loads of force but there won't by any energy.	As above.
59. Jonathan: Uhm, no moving energy.	Jonathan is able to summarize because he has now fully assimilated the definition of energy via work.
60. David: There won't be any energy doing even . . .	Incomplete.
61. Jonathan: There's no energy transferred from one to the other is there?	Now begins to move on to a further concept, accepting what has gone before.

What we have here is a serious and fruitful discussion in which David, Jonathan, and Marianne help one another apply the given definitions to a new case. They make mistakes, but they address themselves to the task in a purposive and rational manner. In understanding that this is so we have often to detach our awareness of the style of speech from the content. Although the conversations are often informal in tone and—in comparison with a written textbook—pursue an indirect path, this should not prevent us from appreciating that a necessary kind of learning is going on.

The Makings of Collaboration

The two examples so far quoted show groups working so successfully that they hardly encourage the reader to ask: what do students have to be able to do in order to construct knowledge jointly in this way; how do they set about contributing to the discussion, and how do they receive what others say? How do they invite contributions from others, and how do they interrelate or reconcile different viewpoints?

We shall now examine in more detail the moves that make up the complex discussions we have been considering. In these two short examples we found these moves being made:

initiating discussion of a new issue	Group 4 No. 1
qualifying another person's contribution	4

implicitly accepting a qualification	5
extending a previous contribution	6
asking for an illustration to test a generalization	Group 1 No.48
providing an example	51
using evidence to challenge an assertion	53
reformulating one's own previous assertion	54

This list ignores social functions such as encouragement—which we will discuss later—and also those more indefinable moves which cannot be summed up in a phrase. Examples of such complex moves can be found in Group 1's utterances, Nos. 56 and 59, in which the two boys summarize the distinction so far arrived at in the discussion.

Elsewhere in our materials we have noted pupils:

obtaining information from others

completing unfinished utterances

encouraging others to continue

inviting others to contribute

repeating with modifications

supporting another's assertion with evidence

We grouped these different moves into four broad categories: initiating, eliciting, extending, and qualifying. When we worked on our transcripts and recordings with these categories in mind, they provided evidence of many collaborative skills shown by thirteen-year-olds. Without such moves, purposive group discussion oriented towards learning would not take place. Some examples of the skills belonging to the four categories are discussed next.

Initiating

We first illustrate how a new perspective is initiated, using mainly examples which follow a pause in the talk. Our first examples are taken from discussions of the task which we call *Vandalism*, though it was in fact concerned with the reasons why some adolescent boys join in gang violence: the groups were given as their starting point part of a transcript of an interview with a former gang leader called Ron.

In Group 1 (which the reader has already met in the science discussion) David begins with: "I think the causes of vandalism, er's, boredom usually, isn't it, can't find anything to do." This is received with giggles and embarrassed silence so he tries again:

> I think the area you live in, er, could affect the way they behave be-
> cause when there's other gangs around you, I think it, er, you
> know, makes you want to fight too if you see them all, fighting and
> that, it looks like fun and so he'll just join in.

And this time the lead is taken up by the others.

It seems important that one member of the group should take the initiative and set up a frame of reference which will enable dis-cussion to begin. Group 4 had little difficulty in finding leads: even Jeanette's cryptic opening is quickly developed:

13. Jeanette: I don't think there's any need for all this fighting do you, but it can cause, cause harm.

14. Bill: Oh, they just go looking for it.

15. Jeanette: Yes, I know.

16. Bill: Well not just so. . . .

Jeanette's initiative has been taken up by Bill, and the other two join in a few moments later.

Later in the same discussion an initiative by Bill meets a chilly fate:

35. Bill: I don't think this last sentence in the interview with Ron is very—useful. I don't think it belongs there. I don't think it's any use at all to the story.

But there the matter is left: the others are unable, or unwilling to take it up.

Many initiating moves are introduced by "I think" or "I don't think," which appears to indicate that as the speaker is raising a new topic, he regards its relevance and usefulness as open to the others' judgment. Initiating moves do sometimes occur without the "I think" introduction, but they are then usually linked closely to the task set to the group. For example, one boy in a discussion of the *Work and Energy* topic revived the talk after a pause by the follow-ing: "Another energy change would be, erm, heat from the sun, erm, helping to produce flowers." One might surmise that in this case the new issue followed so closely the pattern laid down in the task that he did not use "I think" because he did not regard its relevance as open to negotiation or question.

Another case occurred when Group 4 was attempting a task which we have not so far mentioned. Group members were given a draft of a letter supposedly written by a boy, Steve, to his employer in order to break off temporary employment. The task was to reconsider the abrasive tone of the letter in the light of the possibility that Steve might later want further employment. After talking for some minutes, Group 4 fell silent and Jeanette initiated further discussion by quoting a sentence from the original letter:

26. Jeanette: "You must think I'm crazy trying this one on me."	Quotes from the letter a sentence not yet discussed, but does not set up any framework for approaching it.
27. Pauline: I think that's all right. (i.e., that sentence can stand.)	Accepts the proffered focus, and sets up a framework of general approval/disapproval for discussing the sentence.

Jeanette was not offering an opinion but merely—in a very open way—putting forward a focus for attention. It is Pauline who is committing herself to an approach and who therefore uses the "I think."

Exchanges are often initiated by questions, many of these arising directly from the task set. When Group 4 is working on the *Work and Energy* topic, members move on to a new example, thus:

25. Jeanette: Well what do you think about (b) heat to movement in a steam engine?	Invites a lead from one of the others by reading aloud one of the given questions.
27. Bill: I think that, erm, well that's . . (etc.)	Takes up the offered initiative.

In contrast with this, Group 3, having talked for a while about questions set to them on Steinbeck's novel *The Pearl*, turn to a question of its own: "Do you think the book's any good so far?" (Once again, "Do you think?" acknowledges the offering of the initiative.)

Eliciting

It is now time, however, to move from the initiating of discussions to the more generally important matter of how groups sustain coherent talk, and particularly how they invite one another to contribute. Without some such mutual support it seems unlikely that a group could sustain the uncertainties of a focused discussion for any length of time. We shall distinguish four kinds of eliciting moves:

- requests to someone to continue what they are saying;
- requests to expand a previous remark;
- requests for support for the speaker's opinion;
- requests for information.

Simple invitations to continue are rare in the discussions, perhaps because they are potentially claims to a leadership role. In Group 4's discussion of Steve's letter, Alan begins:

28. Alan: Yes, I think you could start off like, erm—

and when he pauses, Bill's, "Go on, go on," encourages him to continue.

More frequently invitations to continue are for explicit purposes. By the time we reached the recording of the *Steve's Letter* discussion, Group 4 members were giving one another a great deal of support: this was not a matter of agreeing with one another, but of attending closely to what was said and replying appropriately:

106. Pauline: I think he should just leave it: "Dear Sir, You must think I'm crazy trying this one on me. Just light work. Do you think clearing up spit, ice cream and fag ends is easy work? You can keep it."

107. Alan: Why, is that what you'd write?

108. Pauline: Yes. Because it's short and it's telling him, it's telling him right from the start.

Alan's question seems to be not so much an expression of surprise as a request for Pauline to extend what she had said so as to confirm his interpretation of her meaning; this is probably because she was still using the abrasive tone of the original letter and this ran counter to much of what had been previously said in the discussion. The question "Is that what you'd write?" contains implicitly not only a request for confirmation, but also for some justification: a mere "yes" might have appeared stubborn or even aggressive, though this would depend upon its intonation.

A slightly different request for expansion occurred when Group 5 attempted the *Bird's Eggs* task, in which the pupils were required to break the shell of an egg, discuss what they observed, and answer questions which included, "Do you think a bird's egg could be fertilized inside the hen's body?" "What makes you think so?"

102. Donald: It's fertilized in the body, it must be. Of course it's fertilized in the body.

103. Louise: What makes you think so?

104. Helen: It must be.

105. David: Because it wouldn't get back through.

106. Helen: It can hardly get through the damn shell, can it?

Louise uses the question from the task card, "What makes you think so?" as if it were her own, and thereby draws a useful reply from Helen at 106. Here the request to expand the previous assertion is explicitly a request for a rational argument in support of it. (This kind of eliciting move is the reciprocal of the *extending* move which will be discussed below, though the latter frequently occurs without having been explicitly elicited.)

The next form of eliciting move to be illustrated is the request for *support*. It is necessary to distinguish the general, almost habitual, appeals for confirmation from more particular ones. Throughout our materials we find frequent examples of statements followed by tag-questions of the "isn't it?", "hasn't he?", "won't they?" kind. For example: "Yes, well, the ground isn't strong enough really, is it?" These often appear to be requests for reassurance that the channel is open and the audience attending, though when they occur at the end of an utterance they may signal *Over to you* to the other participants. These general appeals, in conjunction with nods and eye movements and sounds such as *mm*, undoubtedly play an important part in sustaining conversation. Here, however, we wish to place our emphasis upon appeals which, although often similar in form, operate as direct requests for explicit confirmation or denial of the statement. Group 1, discussing *National Parks*, shows this example:

89. Jonathan: "We don't want any petrol stations, or not many, do we?"

Jonathan makes a firm statement, qualifies it uncertainly, and then asks for support.

90. Barbara: "No, you have them in the villages as well."

Barbara indicates agreement and supplies supporting evidence.

The last kind of eliciting move differs from the others in being a request for *information* and is often quite explicitly focused. Nevertheless, like the other kinds it tends to strengthen the group members' sense of controlling the knowledge which they are using since it ascribes validity to their own existing bodies of knowledge. As might be expected, such requests were particularly frequent in the discussions of *The Pearl* since those pupils who had read further held information not available to the others. One example of this comes from Group 3:

3. Robert: That doctor really cheats him because once he hears about the pearl that Kino's found, he changes his mind about coming to see Coyotito, doesn't he?

4. Margaret: He changes his mind.

5. Robin: Is it him who tries to pinch it when he's asleep?

Robin, who has not read as much of the novel as he should have done, is asking for help in linking the doctor with another incident in the book. The construction of a common interpretation plays an important part in adolescents' discussions of literature, and this is often initiated by similar requests for the elucidation of links between episodes.

In the absence of a teacher the members have has no source of knowledge but themselves and whatever materials, apparatus, or information has been put in front of them. As a result, their behavior is very different from the typical behavior of students in class: they consult the materials rather than watching for signals from a teacher; they test the interpretations which they have put forward by matching them with their existing sense of how things are. In a word, they treat one another as resources.

Extending

When a group found a strategy which appears to be valuable in pursuing the task, members often collaborate to carry it out, so that one takes an up idea from where another left off and extends it. Group 1, while discussing *The Pearl*, turn for a moment to the verisimilitude of that part of the story in which Kino, the pearl-diver, finds the enormous pearl.

49. Marianne: It seems a bit unbelievable, doesn't it?

This continues a foregoing discussion of verisimilitude.

50. David: Yes.

51. Marianne: Really, not realistic enough. He should have. . . .

Interrupted.

52. David: And, er, and, er, as big as his hand.

(Perhaps) Offering part of the reason for scepticism.

53. Marianne: Yes, he should have had a bit more description, not about the pearl but about the actual diving, that he went down, you

Transmutes the judgment of verisimilitude into a demand for description, qualifying it to help the others understand her.

know, and how, what clothes he wore and, you know, what kind of things that he used.

54. Barbara: What he felt when he found it. . . .	Extends the idea towards Kino's subjective experience.
55. Marianne: Yes.	Confirms that Barbara has grasped her intention. (Or merely shows that she is attending?)
56. Barbara: . . . . the shell and that. . . .	Specifies the reference of *it* in 54.
57. David: Well when. . . .	Tries to enter.
58. Marianne: And how long he can hold. . . .	Suggests another detail for the description but is interrupted.
59. David: Well when he came. . . .	Begins to make the contribution attempted at 57.
. . . . Well they described that, how long he held his breath.	Understands Marianne's incomplete remark and deals with it.
When, when he came up and when he, when he slipped a knife into it, it tightened up and he couldn't open it.	Returns to his original idea, which (implicitly) presents an example where Steinbeck had provided realistic detail of the kind required.
60. Marianne: Mm, that were good.	Makes explicit the appreciation implicit in David's contribution.

We have presented this sequence at some length to illustrate how skilfully a group may at best work together in taking up one another's ideas in order to extend them further, or to transmute them. It is not at all unusual for two or three members of a group to construct a sentence jointly. A typical example comes from Group 1's discussion of *National Parks*:

60. Marianne: I think bigger fines should be imposed for the people who don't obey the country laws and thereby spoil the countryside. . . .

21. Jonathan: Yes.

22. Marianne: . . . .by leaving. . . .

23. Jonathan: . . . . by dropping litter. . . .

24. Marianne: . . . . and broken glass.

Qualifying

We will not illustrate further the *extending* function, since it shades imperceptibly into our next category, the *qualifying* function. To add to and extend what someone else has said is inevitably to change it, perhaps to qualify its range of application, or to point out complexities not mentioned in the original statement. Both *extending* and *qualifying* will be illustrated incidentally in many of our quotations, since these moves form the staple of collaborative dialogue. For example, the exchange from Group 1's discussion of *Work and Energy* given at the start of this chapter was composed mainly of such moves. The reader may care to look back at the extract with these categories in mind.

Our first example of *qualifying* comes from a group and a task which have not previously been mentioned. Groups 9 to 16 are smaller than the other groups, each being composed either of three girls or of three boys. The task in question was related to air pressure, and is called *Spaceman*. In a previous science lesson a demonstration had been presented to the class in which a corked bottle had been placed inside a bell jar, and the pressure in the bell jar lowered until the cork was ejected from the bottle. The task was comprised of two questions requiring explanation of the demonstration, and two requiring the pupils to apply the same principle to a spaceship and a spaceman. In the passage to be quoted, members of Group 16 have gone beyond the task and have set themselves a new question: they are considering unasked what would have happened if the pressure inside the bottle had been lower than that around it, instead of higher. They had already agreed that the bottle would *cave in* and continue:

44. Edward: If it had been a plastic bottle it would have been, erm, crushed in, wouldn't it?

> This is the first suggestion that the material of which the bottle is made is likely to affect the outcome.

45. Philip: Yes, but it would have been if it were glass.

46. Harold: Well, the glass one would have probably cracked, wouldn't it?

> Both take up the idea and apply it to glass.

47. Edward: It, it wouldn't . . . If it was thick glass.

> Dissatisfied with Harold's proposition and wishing to qualify it, raises a new issue, the thickness of the vessel's wall.

If it was very, very thin glass like slide glass. . . .	Interrupted.
48. Harold: Or the cork would get sucked in.	Raises an alternative possibility.
49. Edward: Or the cork, er. If it was thick glass. . . .	Accepts Harold's qualification, relating it to the thickness of the glass.
50. Philip: Yes, the cork.	
51. Harold: The cork would get pushed in though, wouldn't it?	Substitutes another formulation for No. 48.
52. Philip: Yes, the cork would also get pushed in then that would mean that the air would have got into the bottle, so it wouldn't have happened.	Attempts to summarize, interrelating what has gone before.
53. Harold: Most likely the cork would get pushed in, rather than the jar smashed.	Agreement reached.
54. Edward: Yes.	

Here the three boys of Group 16 use the talk as an opportunity to interrelate several of the variables that are relevant to explaining the phenomenon considered. They seem to have an intuitive sense of the relevance of the thickness of the vessel's wall, the substance it is made of, and the relation of these to the resistance of the cork, and through discussion are trying to make these explicit in concrete terms. This faces them with considerable problems of assimilation. For example, when at No. 48 Harold puts in the reference to the cork, Edward might well have treated this interruption as a threatening contradiction; the momentum of the discussion however carries the boys on to the point where it has become clear that Harold's contribution is a qualification not a rejection of what went before, and that it is a useful contribution to their account. Similarly, in Group 1's discussion of the *National Parks* task an apparent contradiction leads the group toward a deeper understanding. In order to deal with the various demands on a National Park it is useful—and perhaps essential—to define groups of users with different requirements. This is not immediately obvious to thirteen-year-olds.

46. Marianne: At the roadside there should be a lot of big car parks [parking lots] to accommodate all these visitors and tourists.

Proposes facilities for visitors, but fails to make a distinction between different groups of them.

47. David: Spoil the countryside won't it?

Points out that these facilities may be in conflict with other requirements.

48. Jonathan: Ah, that's what'll stop, erm, stop them from going all over the countryside, won't it?

Suggests that there is no real conflict: the car parks [parking lots] would protect the countryside, not spoil it.

49. David: That's the big one—to stop people going all over.

Identifies Jonathan's point as the central responsibility of national parks.

50. Marianne: But if there's picnic areas. If there's picnic areas then they won't need to go out into the countryside. They'd be able to see it though.

Suggests another device for controlling tourists' use of the parks.

51. Barbara: Yes, but that's it. . . .

Attempts to enter the discussion.

52. David: Yes, but people want to go into the countryside.

Points out that their attempts to protect the parks are ignoring one of their primary purposes, to make the countryside available.

53. Marianne: Not all of them. Just tourists that are passing by. . . .

Marianne begins to make the necessary distinction between tourists and other users of the national parks.

Thus, in dealing with particular issues—the provision of car parks [parking lots] and picnic areas—Group 1 has met with differences of opinion which could only be dealt with by moving from the particular issues to more abstract principles, the range of users and their needs. Crucial in this were David's *qualifying* move, "Yea, but people want to go out into the countryside," and Marianne's reception of this, "Not all of them"; the former showed the group that there was contradiction within what they were saying, and the second showed that a deeper analysis could account for this contradiction. It is worth remembering at this point that these students are thirteen-year-olds of average ability, and that the shift to more abstract levels of analysis illustrated in this example and the previous one represent for them considerable intellectual achievement. In both these cases this shift of level depended upon the recognition of contradictions and the willingness to look for principles that would reconcile the contradictions.

In presenting examples of *initiating, eliciting, extending,* and *qualifying* moves, it has been our intention to show some of the complex skills which younger adolescents command and which they can under encouraging circumstances utilize in the development of understanding. These should not be seen merely as individual skills, however: they exist in group discussions or not at all. These moves are mutually supportive. By taking the trouble to elicit an opinion from someone else, or by utilizing what has been said by extending it further, the group members ascribe meaningfulness to one another's attempts to make sense of the world. This helps them to continue, however hesitantly, with the attempts to shape their own understanding by talking and contrasts sharply with any schooling which reduces the learner to a receiver of authoritative knowledge. It would be misleading, though, not to mention differences of viewpoint. As we have shown earlier in this section, the expression of a dissident opinion, provided it is understood as a qualification and not as a dismissal, plays a crucial part in advances in understanding. The possibility of using differences of opinion constructively rests upon a sense of shared validity, and our next section will be devoted to a consideration of the social skills upon which a sense of shared validity depends.

In discussing the makings of collaboration we have been primarily concerned with students' ability to work together in clarifying their understanding of a given topic. In the next section we shall be concerned with the task management and social skills upon which collaboration is based.

Task Management and Social Skills

For the most part, roles in the informal discussions we recorded were taken up and relinquished without these transitions being explicitly acknowledged by the participants. As we have seen, someone proposes a topic and a frame of reference for approaching it; other persons accept this, or modify it, or put forward an alternative. Sometimes they become aware of straying from the point and therefore redirect the discussion. Eventually someone will either move the discussion to another topic or decide that it is concluded, and the rest of the group will concur. To a great extent, therefore, discussions were shaped tacitly—through the *initiating, eliciting, extending* and *qualifying* moves shown in the last section.

However, there were occasions in the groups' discussions when it became necessary to negotiate certain choices and courses of action publicly. At certain points groups needed to attend to the management of their work—perhaps to agree how to share out jobs or to decide when it was appropriate to move on to the next heading in the task. Occasionally disagreements or conflict might arise, and these would need to be dealt with before the group could progress. A contrasting but equally public feature of some groups at other times was the support offered to encourage different group members to contribute.

In this section we have grouped together examples of cases where such choices are in some way publicly negotiated. This includes: how tasks are controlled and carried out, how group members deal with disagreement and conflict, and how they give support and encouragement. Finally, we wind up this chapter with a discussion of more general differences between groups, giving examples of two contrasting social strategies—*collaborating* and *defending*.

Controlling Progress Through the Tasks

Every group has to control its progress through the given tasks, determine the boundaries of what is to be considered relevant to them, and move at an appropriate moment from one question, or one aspect of the topic, to another. Where the task includes manipulative activities—as with some of the scientific topics—it is necessary for one or more members of the group to carry these out. At the end they have to decide when one member should let the researcher know that the discussion is completed.

For the most part, progress through the task is paced by members of the group reading out another question whenever they feel this to be appropriate. When pupils do this they are usually not *playing the role of the teacher*, since unlike teachers they are not asking questions to which they know the answer in order to test the others' knowledge. Occasionally the question-asking does approximate to a different kind of teaching move, that is, when one of the given questions is used to elicit extended thinking from other members of the group.

Most of the groups went very deliberately through the *Spaceman* questions. Here are the Group 15 boys:

17. Graham: (The pressure inside the corked bottle) was greater than the pressure outside in the bell jar, so it pushed the, er, cork out.

(Summarized here for brevity)

Summarizing and completing a sequence.

18. Barry: Yes, we did that before just, just before didn't we?

Recognizing that it was a summary.

19. Graham: Yes. Number two: why did the cork come out?

Moving on to a new topic by reading given question.

Well, we've done that, haven't we?

Seeking agreement for a move on to the third question.

20. Barry: Yes, we've done that. We've now done two, Tape.

Explicit acceptance. Addresses to the tape recorder information about their progress.

It should be made clear that this level of self-awareness was not common: Barry's last remark suggests that the presence of the tape recorder may have played some part in this.

Other tasks, however, were not composed of a tightly-structured series of questions as the *Spaceman* task was, and this made the control of relevance a different matter. There was not a great deal of obvious irrelevance in the discussions of topics such as *The Pearl* or *Vandalism*, but the group's attention often moved from one sub-topic to another without explicit conclusions being formulated. (We are not necessarily regarding this as unhelpful to learning.) Very occasionally members of the group became aware of this and attempted to focus the discussion. During their talk about *The Pearl*, for example, Group 1 put forward *the doctor* as an example of evil in the story:

87. David: The doctor were a bit evil though, wasn't he?

88. Barbara: Yes.

89. Marianne: He's, he's. . . .

90. David: His big fat, his fat, nose.

91. Barbara: Yes, I can imagine him.

92. David: Yes, his big fat, his fat and always smoking big cigars and that. He won't, he won't cure anybody.

93. Marianne: Living in towns and that.

94. Marianne: What about the good things, what would you say the good things were?

It seems Marianne has judged that the discussion of evil had been satisfactorily concluded, so that it was appropriate to direct attention to *the good things*. This was a quotation from the given task: "Discuss among yourselves what you have found in the story so far—the 'good and bad things, the black and white things and good and evil things' as Steinbeck says." The set task goes on to mention characters, setting and the way the book is written but finally gives the pupils the responsibility of deciding what is worth discussing. In the sequence quoted above, Group 1 is guided by the quotation, though in the discussion as a whole this group and the others range widely.

When it comes to ending the whole discussion, groups often reach agreement by non-verbal signals. In some cases, however, there was explicit consultation to decide whether they had finished the task: in ending their discussion of *Gang Violence* (a variant of the *Vandalism* task), Sheila says, "I mean, I think we've had enough now of this so I think we'll tell her, eh?" and goes to tell the researcher that they have finished. A more sophisticated version comes at the end of Group 4's long and exhaustive discussion of *Steve's Letter*. Jeanette says, "Well, I think we've covered all the main points." Bill replies, "Yes" and someone switches off the tape recorder: they are aware of having completed a successful discussion.

Group 15 was unusually explicit in bringing its two discussions to a conclusion. In the *Spaceman* task, they had discussed each of the given questions and raised several issues of their own when Barry asked, "I think we've finished now, do you?" There is then some joking about avoiding a lesson, and Alec says:

62. Alec: Erm, shall we go over it again?

63. Barry: No, we've been through it and all that. We know what happened.

But Alex insists on recapitulating their answers to the questions and this takes them on to further discussion of their own about pressure in the sea. Eventually Graham asks, "I think we've finished now, don't you?" and although the others agree, they continue talking for a while about a *pressure pill* in a James Bond film. Members of Group 15 enjoy talking and are able to make negotiated decisions about how they do it. In this they contrast markedly with the girls of Group 9 who went through the questions three times in a worried search for right answers.

Allocating Activities

When a group has not only to control its progress through the given questions, but also manipulate materials and apparatus, allocating tasks to one another, this presents special problems. We shall see later how some groups were almost entirely prevented from discussion by the requirement to make holes in eggshells—without breaking them. One set of three boys however successfully collaborated in managing the apparatus upon which the task called *Carbon Dioxide in Water* was based.

To understand the social problem (rather than the scientific one) it is only necessary to know that one member of the group had to blow into a tube while the others observed the effect of this upon two containers of lime water. (The boys are Robert and Robin of Group 3 and Bill of Group 4; they were timetabled together for science.) Bill begins by claiming the role of blower by saying, "Right, I'll breathe." Robert observes what happens and the two of them discuss what they see. In the course of this Bill moves the discussion on:

6. Bill: Now there's the question there. Why does the apparatus only let air in through one tube and only let air out through the other?

Signals change of focus. Quotes question verbatim.

7. Robert: Well it, it would suck it, it would suck it, wouldn't it?

Attempts an explanation.

8. Bill: Hold it.

(Difficult to interpret. Perhaps handing over the blowing tube.)

9. Robert: Let's have a look. (Bubbling noises).

10. Robert: That's because when you blow through it, it can't. . . . the air can't. . . . the air pushes it up in there, doesn't it. . . . the air pushes down on that. . . .

Takes on role of blower. Attempts an explanation.

11. Bill: Do it again.

Asks for another opportunity to observe.

These two boys manage easily to pass the manipulative task to and fro, to decide the sequencing of activities, and to share in explaining. This undoubtedly is made easier for them by Robin's willingness to stand back and observe, though this prevents us from knowing how far he understands the phenomenon.

Dealing with Competition and Conflict

In an earlier section we illustrated how the young people in the groups dealt with the need to qualify what others had said, and to accept such qualification of their own statements. When they are able to treat such qualification as a contribution to the group's common thinking and not as a rejection of themselves, no conflict arises. But there are occasions when conflict does arise and needs to be coped with; here we shall examine only occasions when it is done successfully.

Members of Group 4 are particularly skillful at dealing with potential social difficulties, and this skill seems to be shared by all four members of the group. Two of them have been rapidly drafting an alternative form of *Steve's Letter*, and Alan asks Bill to read his draft, even though he has not completed it.

130. Alan: What have you got so far, Bill?

131. Jeanette: Erm, wait a minute, let him finish his first. You read yours, Pauline [*read* is in the present tense].

132. Pauline: Well, I've put nearly the same as you. [And so on. . . .]

Jeanette manages to head off the interruption to Bill, who is still writing, and instead induces Pauline, who has finished her draft, to read it.

In the next example Group 4 is coping with a substantial difference of opinion. At the beginning of the discussion of *Steve's Letter*, the girls Pauline and Jeanette wish the latter's angry tone to be retained, whereas the boys Bill and Alan want to soften it, because it *sounds disrespectful* and may prevent future employment. After some discussion they are still divided.

92. Bill: If he wants another job I wouldn't put, *I wouldn't be seen dead in the place.* It's just asking for trouble, isn't it?	Bill wishes to delete one of the more obviously offensive phrases.
93. Alan: No, it, it's a bit, it's a bit, it's a bit on the. . . .	Trying to frame his objections in moderate terms.
94. Pauline: Well I don't think he should put so much because really he's just, he's just wanting his attention and say, say ah well he'll give me the job back if I, if I start making trouble for him. He should just put a few words and leave it at that, I think.	Introduces new viewpoint, in effect asking the group to consider the overall purpose of the letter.
95. Bill: Yes, well. . . .	Message received.

96. Alan: In some ways I suppose so. . . .

Again a tactful concession of validity to another's views.

97. Bill: If you put down, if you put down, *Dear Sir, Thank you for inviting me to this, er, job. . . .*

Sets up an alternative version for ironical purposes.

98. Pauline: . . . .but.

97. Bill (cont'd): *but I, I enjoyed it very much.* Well that's telling a complete lie and he's going to give you it next year and you're not going to get any, any more improvements you know.

Makes clear the justification for including an explicit statement of the poor job conditions.

99. Jeanette: At least he tells the truth.

100. Bill: Yes.

Reaffirming her original view (that the letter should express the writer's feelings without inhibition).

101. Jeanette: He doesn't keep it to himself.

102. Alan: I know but he doesn't have to say in that, so many words really.

Concedes validity of Jeanette's views but qualifies them. (Tell the truth in a tactful way.)

103. Bill: No, he could, he could be a bit more res, he could be more respectful.

Agrees with Alan's qualification.

104. Alan: Yes, yes, that's that's more the word, really because, erm, say he might be an old man, a friend like. . . .(and so on)

Accepts Bill's suggestion, and goes on to put forward a new consideration (the effect of the letter upon recipient).

This exchange is not untypical of how, in a discussion that is going well, a group will cope with disagreement. It would be a mistake to overemphasize Alan's conciliatory moves, though they may well have played some part in Group 4's exceptional cohesiveness. It is well to note, however, that at least some thirteen-year-olds can work to hold a group together while differences of opinion are being expressed: Alan is not the only member of our groups to make such moves. More important probably is the willingness of Group 4 members to take one another's views seriously even when they disagree with them, and this willingness is clearly demonstrated whenever they counter another opinion with a relevant objection to it, as happens throughout Group 4's discussion of *Steve's Letter*. It is possible, however, that other groups use gesture and tone of voice to indicate their attentiveness to alternative views. It would be misleading to suggest that this can only be done by verbally explicit means.

To say that the members of Group 4 work well together is not to say that they are mealy-mouthed; in the next exchange, which comes from their *National Parks* discussion, Alan himself issues a sharp challenge. Alan has suggested that hotels be built for the clubs that use the national park:

78. Pauline: Yes, but they don't need these. I mean they can get these anywhere else.

79. Alan: Why not? Why don't they need them?

80. Pauline: Well, they don't. I mean this is where they go to. . . .

81. Alan: Bill, Bill, say if you put hotels—now listen here you—say if these are your hotels, there'll be loads, there'll be loads of people coming won't there? It'll be like a big fairground.

Alan puts his challenge forcefully and equally forcefully insists that Bill listen to the counter-argument. Yet no personal rejection is implied in the forcefulness; indeed, both the challenge and the insistence imply that the others' opinions matter.

We now reach the edge of overt conflict, and this often arises from some boy or girl who has a more aggressive style. Margaret in Group 3 typically asks questions as if she were making an assertion:

16. Margaret: Hey up, here it says, er, national parks provide, er, swimming. Why do they want swimming pools then, eh?

Her tone of voice makes this a dogmatic assertion, but the group is able to contain her aggressiveness, and later, after a repetition, she has her reply.

23. Robert: Yes, well the people, well most people don't like swimming in lakes because they think they're dirty.

24. Christine: Yes, they are.

Jokes are of considerable importance to all of the groups in coping with strong feelings such as anger and disgust. The *Bird's Eggs* task led to a great deal of joking, Group 5 being particularly inventive: "It's gone all over my shoes. I'm the only kid in our class with yolk-flavoured shoes. Look at them." And another member of the group: "Somebody cracked a yolk." On some occasions social pressure is put upon group members in a joking manner. Group 4 is discussing

Work and Energy; for a while it has been Alan who has carried the main weight of the explaining, with little more than supportive noises from the others, but then everyone falls silent for several seconds, long enough for them to become aware of a hiatus. Alan, who apparently feels that others should share the responsibility of keeping the talk going, is here far from conciliatory, and breaks the silence by asking in an elaborately artificial voice:

41. Alan: What do you think of, what do you think about this question, Bill? Is work always done when energies change in form?

The others laugh loudly, probably appreciating that this is an oblique way of compelling Bill to take more responsibility. Bill replies:

42. Bill: No, not always. It depends what you'd classify as work.

And the discussion develops seriously thereafter, with Bill playing a central part in it. Alan has succeeded in manipulating the allocation of social roles without appearing to claim the right to do so, and—as far as one can tell—without giving offense. The possibility of sustained discussion of the topic in hand depends upon allocating roles and responsibilities—an entirely necessary disposition—without spending excessive time upon dispute or decision making.

Supportive Behavior

It was characteristic of the more successful discussions that members of the groups sometimes asked questions solely in order to bring in contributions from others, either from awareness that they had been silent for a while or from interest in the other's opinion. We are not referring here to initiating moves like those already illustrated, but to those which are addressed to a particular person. The following example comes from Group 4's discussion of *The Pearl*, while they are talking in general terms about their responses to the novel.

42. Bill: But you've got to pay, you've got to pay attention to it or you miss something that goes on.

43. Alan: Yes. What do you think about it, Pauline?

The opening "Yes" of Alan's utterance seems to operate as a *message received* signal to Bill, so that the coming change of direction will not appear to reject his contribution. Then, aware that Pauline has not spoken for a while, he tries to bring her in with an invitation which is in effect a blank check to contribute.

A parallel example occurs in Group 1's discussion of *The Pearl*. The group has been working together to describe the village where the events take place when there is a short pause and a change of direction.

115. Barbara: Go on then, you start. . . .

116. Marianne: Em, what do you think that'll hap, happen, later on in the book when we've read it, you know, what will happen to the pearl and the doctor and everything?

Barbara is willing to step back and give room to Marianne, thus allowing her to initiate a new strategy which proves to be very profitable.

We have found no shortage of such moves in those discussions which have given lengthy attention to the assigned topic and would hypothesize that mutual support of this kind plays an important part in sustaining attention. It is not merely the acknowledgment of a common purpose by members of the group: more importantly, when one replies to another person's remark in careful detail, one is assigning significance and validity to it. Even disagreement, if it is rationally argued and not merely dismissive, will not be interpreted as aggression by the person to whom it is addressed but will rather reinforce his or her sense of collaborating in the meaningful construction of knowledge.

The support implicit in attending seriously to another's opinion may in educational contexts be the form of support most likely to influence learning. Nevertheless, thirteen-year-old boys and girls have at their disposal more explicit means of giving support, though most use them infrequently. (It is worth noting that what we are calling social skills, and especially supportive behavior, are very poorly represented in Groups 9 to 16, who met only on the one occasion, in comparison particularly with Groups 1 and 4 who developed a corporate identity.) The means available include the expression of agreement, praise, explicit reference to others' contributions, expressions of positive feeling about what is being achieved, and naming one another (though naming can be used for other purposes). In this section we illustrate these five kinds of supportive behavior.

Formal expressions of agreement. Formal expressions of agreement, which are not very common, appear to occur mainly during the opening moments of discussion, when all members of the group are eager to encourage fluent talk. Group 1 begins its discussion of *National Parks* thus:

1. David: I think that they should put these facilities, er, by the roadside and not spoil the countryside, you know.

2. Marianne: Yes, I agree with you.

It seems likely that Marianne is not so much enthusiastic about David's suggestion as wishing to encourage his initiative in proposing an initial frame of reference. Similarly Group 4's discussion of *Work and Energy* begins with a statement by Bill to which Alan replies: "Yes, I agree with you there, Bill." This is followed by a pause. It seems likely that these expressions of agreement are useful only when the group have not yet lost their self-awareness in the talk.

Naming. It is not easy to generalize about naming. The use of Bill's name by Alan in the above example seems to be part of the rather self-conscious determination to open lines of communication which has just been commented on. In the previous section, however, we looked at an occasion when Alan named Bill in order to persuade him to take part in the discussion, and our transcriptions contained another similar example. The importance of naming—when it is not concerned with forcing participation—is that to address a remark to someone by name implies an interest in his or her opinion, which is likely to encourage a reply. In Group 9, Catherine is talking about spacemen returning to earth, and wants to enlist the support of Shirley.

95. Catherine: They go through a certain space, I don't know how much it is. . . .

96. Shirley: What?

97. Catherine: It presses them down, doesn't it, Shirley? It presses them down when they're coming through the air.

98. Shirley: Mm.

Here the naming seems to be part of the appeal for support.

Sometimes the effect of naming is to imply that disagreement with another's opinion does not imply a rejection of that person. Here Group 2 is discussing *The Pearl*:

52. Sylvia: Yes, but I suppose if they got a pearl like that they'd spend it on daft things and all.

53. Audrey: No I don't think so.

54. Sylvia: I wouldn't be surprised, I wouldn't be surprised if they did.

55. Audrey: I don't think so Sylvia.

In this case the naming partly performed the function of catching the attention of the person addressed but at the same time serves to express to her an interest in her opinion and its justification, ensuring that disagreement is not interpreted as personal rejection.

Reference back. As might be expected in informal discussion, explicit reference back to what another member has said earlier is not common. This is not to say that they do not take up and utilize others' ideas, both those which have just been expressed and others from much earlier in the discussion: most groups did this freely. What we are concerned with here is the acknowledgment of such indebtedness by an explicit reference to the source of the opinion, even where it is referred to in order to be qualified or contradicted. As might be expected from their display of other social skills Group 4 provides us with an example, this one from their discussion of the evil doctor in *The Pearl*:

22. Alan: It said that, er, if you've got some money he'll do it, but if you haven't he won't do it, so he's just after the money really like you said Jeanette.

This reference back to an earlier remark by Jeanette adds little to the meaning of what is being said, but with other social moves is important in knitting this group together in defining their responses to the novel.

A contrasting example comes from Group 2's discussion of *The Pearl*:

60. Audrey: You, you can believe, that, there are people like this in the world, and you can believe this story, because the way the author, writes it down, the way he describes them. . . .

61. Sylvia: I suppose you've got a point there but, erm, I don't think, er, I don't like the village and that that it's set in.

The introductory phrase, "I suppose you've got a point there" concedes to Audrey's point of view before Sylvia goes on to express her dislike of the village setting. The softening phrase is a signal to Audrey that Sylvia values her participation in the discussion and does not wish to reject her in voicing her alternative opinion.

Explicit praise. Explicit praise of others' contributions is very infrequent indeed, though Group 4 gives an example. Pauline has just said that if hotels are provided in national parks they should not be so frequent as to "litter it up," and Bill responds: "Yes, that a, that's a good idea." Such ready appreciation of their suggestions plays its part in sustaining Group 4's exceptional ability to stay with a topic, exploring it from various points of view.

Expressions of shared feeling. One would expect that members of any group thus committed to collaborative discussion would support themselves with expressions of shared feeling. Several groups expressed satisfaction at what they had achieved by the end of their discussion. It is Group 1 members who express most clearly their empathy with one another; and especially during their discussion of *The Pearl* which clearly gave them pleasure. This satisfaction is twice expressed by David, first in appreciation of the recreation by Marianne of part of the story.

98. Marianne: But the writer keeps mentioning in the story about the music that comes into Kino's ears, doesn't he? You know, the family music and then it's the evil music that comes when, when the scorpion's there, it's evil music playing in his ears. I think I like that, you know.

99. David: Shuper.

The relish with which David re-experiences Steinbeck's metaphor is richly embodied in his tone of voice, so that the listener is aware of a warmth with which this group is able to share the recollected experience. And at the end of the discussion he sums up the group's sense of a job well done with the same word, "Shuper," which in context seems reinforced by his idiosyncratic pronunciation of the word.

Collaborating or Defending

Our concern lies not with social skills for their own sake but only with the extent to which they contribute to a group's ability to learn from discussion. Each group is simultaneously negotiating social relationships and attempting the given task: if the former preempts their time and attention, little learning will go on. For this reason we have tried to understand how the students cope with social relationships and with the allocation of roles, and therefore with the allocation of power over the progress of the discussion. Much of this negotiation goes on through intonation, facial expression, and bodily posture and gestures: in focusing attention upon those social moves which are put into words, we are implicitly treating these as representative of the other less accessible moves and may therefore be misrepresenting the whole. It may well be, for example, that when a group is smoothly constructing an interpretation of the given task, there is no need for relationships to be negotiated explicitly. Therefore, we wish in this section to consider the group's social strategies more generally.

To distinguish a productive from a defensive approach to a task we next compare exchanges from two groups' discussion of the *Causes of Vandalism* task. (They had been given extracts from a transcribed interview with Ron, the former leader of a boys' gang, and were asked in general terms to discuss the causes of gang violence and vandalism. This should be distinguished from the variant of this task—called *Gang Violence*—given to Groups 9 to 16.) In both cases the exchange quoted comes from near the beginning of the recording; they have been chosen not for the content of what is said, but to illustrate the difference in the two groups' approaches. The first example comes from Group 1:

3. David: I think the area you live in, er, could affect the way they behave because when there's other gangs around you, I think it, er, you know, makes you want to fight too. If you see them all, fighting and that, it looks like fun and so he'll just join in.

> An initiating move to start the discussion.
>
> Links the general issue with the particular case of Ron.

4. Jonathan: Yes, he only, only, he'll only start fighting if other people do.

> Accepts David's lead and extends it.

5. Marianne: And he thinks that the only way he can make himself, big, and make himself a somebody, is to prove to people that he is, big and is, tough and fight, and can fight all the time.

> Further extends this line of thought by reminding the group of Ron's need for self-display.

6. David: Well he wasn't, he wasn't very tough at school was he and no, nobody like. . . .

> Both David and Marianne are inventing realistic supportive detail, none of which is given in the task materials.

7. Marianne: No, his parents, his parents were always hitting him. . . .

8. David: Nobody liked him did they, so he wanted to make himself right big by beating everybody up, so he'd be famous.

> Further extending the construction of Ron's motives.

9. Marianne: And he isn't really brainy so he had to do it in a different way. . . . (etc.)

> Qualifying the foregoing with a further insight.

In this exchange we have no explicit supportive moves of the kinds discussed above, but instead close attentiveness to what has gone before, so that each utterance is closely linked to its predecessors.

This becomes partly overt in the linking phrases, "Yes, he only. . . .", "And he thinks. . . .", "Well, he wasn't. . . ." and so on, but more significant is the closeness with which the content of each utterance is related to what has preceded it.

We do not want to misrepresent our material by suggesting that none of the groups had any difficulties in working together on the given tasks. In the next example, which contrasts greatly with the previous one, Group 3, working on the same task, find it hard to start in on its work because the members cannot establish a social framework for collaboration. Here social difficulties impede engagement with learning and produce a defensive rather than a collaborative exchange. Robert has begun by rejecting the idea that young people engage in vandalism because they "aren't given enough things to do."

5. Robert: Oh I, I don't, I, I think it's partly that, but you get some people that, really want to be vandals, really want to smash things up just for the pleasure of it, and you get some that haven't anything better to do so they just go around smashing things up.	Puts forward two parallel explanations.
It's a bit daft really, isn't it. . . .?	Invites others to join in.
6. Christine: Say something, Margaret. *(Whispered)*	Primarily concerned with whether the other girl is doing a fair share.
7. Margaret: You haven't said anything yet. *(Whispered)*	As above.
8. Christine: I've said, yes, yes. *(Whispered)*	As above.
9. Robert: Do you think Ron's any good?	Tries to initiate a new strategy.
10. Christine: No.	A minimal response.
11. Margaret: Do you think Ron's what?	Aggressive tone: sounds like a refusal to contribute.
12. Christine: He doesn't give, he doesn't give good answers.	Tries to respond to Robert's initiating move (No. 9).
13. Robert: No, he just said that he	Interrupted.

wanted to be somebody. He could
have been somebody if he worked
hard couldn't he, instead of. . . .

14. Margaret: Yes, but not like that.   ?

15. Robert: Instead of, he always   Completing his previous contribu-
wanted to make people be fright-   tion.
ened of him.

Although this is a topic about which most adolescents have plenty
to say, Group 3 is making little progress. Robert is trying to get the
discussion going, while the two girls block his attempts by squab-
bling or by refusing to accept his leads or (later in the recording) by
making fun. The other boy joins in later, but only when forced to do
so by one of the girls. Later in the discussion Robert too does not listen to the others and interrupts them, ignoring their contributions
and failing to address them or ask them for elucidation.

Perhaps they suffer from shyness, or do not like one another, or
resent being recorded, or are not interested in the subject, or dislike
school; the reasons for their failure to work together need not concern us at this moment. In contrast with the members of Group 1,
they are not attending closely to one another. There is no sense of
common purpose and no sign of encouragement, but rather of aggression and self-protection.

This negative case may come as a shock after the many examples of constructive collaboration we have given above. Our purpose in citing it is to acknowledge the problems which some students may encounter: collaboration and learning do not necessarily
follow when small groups of students are asked to work together. In
this instance, the students showed too much distrust of one another
and the context to find collaboration possible.

It is unlikely that the members of Group 3 lacked the social
means to collaborate that we have been discussing in this chapter.
However, here and in other recordings, they did not use them as frequently as did Groups 1 and 4. Rather, they seemed too concerned
with some potential threat to be able to take the risks necessary to
participate in shared, exploratory talk of this kind. Confidence in
oneself and trust in others seem to be a necessary condition for collaboration.

We found such confidence and trust more commonly in those
groups that worked together for some time in making recordings
and it led to the development of shared meanings that we have documented in this chapter. As researchers, we only observed, but as
teachers, we would have intervened at this point to help Group 3

make something more positive of their work. For these three constructively to take part in group discussion it would be necessary to involve them in finding a topic and a social context that would be meaningful to them, perhaps to design a task with a tighter structure and pre-allocation of roles. Such issues of task design are taken up in more detail in Chapter 4, with a view to helping teachers provide the frameworks that support collaboration.

Working Together "To Good Purpose"

In this chapter we have sought to clarify the makings of collaboration in small group discussion. The extracts we have quoted demonstrate that school students of average ability can work together in small groups to good purpose, engaging with tasks set by the teacher and managing them through to completion.

More than this, these extracts show that school students can develop a complex array of collaborative competences which they use to support joint exploration of the topic at hand. Initiation of topics and sub-topics, extension of nascent ideas and arguments, and qualitative evaluation of these developing lines of thought and the elicitation of further contributions to take the flow of ideas further—these are the core strands of this collaboration. The chapter also shows students displaying an impressive array of social skills which were needed to manage the progress of the small group discussions, including negotiating interpersonal relationships, participation, disagreements and conflicting views. The dialogic articulation and interrelation of different points of view which is the crucible of learning becomes a real possibility in group discussions such as these.

In the next chapter we shift focus to examine the cognitive strategies that learners used. Subsequently, in Chapter 4, we will draw out the implications of the materials presented in Chapters 2 and 3 for teachers seeking to implement small group discussions in their own classrooms.

Chapter Three

Cognitive Strategies and Reflection in the Groups

Collaboration is necessary—but on its own it is not enough. We were interested in group talk that would lead to the construction of understanding. At the micro-level, we found in our materials a range of logical relationships which might link the thinking expressed in an utterance to that expressed in its predecessors, for instance:

1. Proposes a cause
2. Proposes a result
3. Expands loosely (e.g., adds descriptive details)
4. Applies a principle to a case
5. Categorizes
6. States conditions under which statement is valid or invalid
7. Advances evidence
8. Negates
9. Evaluates
10. Puts alternative view
11. Suggests a method
12. Restates in different terms

This list may well not be exhaustive and the logical relationships used clearly depend upon the given task; in *Work and Energy*, for example, there were many examples of *applies a principle to a case*, whereas in *Causes of Vandalism* there were many examples of *ex-*

pands loosely. Most of these twelve logical relationships can easily be identified in the examples given in the previous chapter.

Collaboration and Strategy

Although these logical categories can be used to describe the relationship between two utterances in terms of links between ideas, they do not show what these utterances are contributing to the development of a line of thought. When the students made a contribution to discussion they did so in pursuit of a purpose that shaped the cognitive strategy they adopted. It was this strategy that determined the logical relationships. When a student *proposed a cause* she did so (for example) in order to put forward a hypothetical explanation for the others to test; when one *advanced evidence* he or she was probably supporting or qualifying a previous assertion. Talk is a matter of *doing things with words*: we needed to identify *cognitive strategies* (such as offering a hypothesis or using evidence to support an assertion) which would represent the purposes that directed the talk and thereby shaped the development of new ways of understanding. We found it more useful to identify the cognitive strategies than to focus attention upon logical relationships, which proved to be too static and restricted in scale for our purposes. The course of a discussion is directed by a tacit interplay between the perceptions and purposes of participants; identifying cognitive strategies enabled us to direct attention to the purposes that shaped the students' discussion over a sequence of utterances and to capture the significant shifts from one to another, for it is these that make is possible to understand how discussion contributes to learning.

In this chapter we illustrate the cognitive strategies adopted by the groups we studied, how they (*a*) constructed the question that they were to answer, (*b*) raised new questions of their own, (*c*) set up hypotheses, (*d*) used evidence to check the validity of an assertion and (*e*) expressed feelings and recreated experience. In the chapter's final section we go on to discuss the extent to which the students showed awareness of and reflected on what they were saying and doing.

Constructing the Question

It would be a mistake to think that when the set task, typed on cards, has been put into the hands of the students in a group that they yet *know what the question is.* To turn the typed words into something which can be answered, it is necessary for members of the group to *construct the question* by using what they know already to make sense of it. In some cases, our groups had already spent lesson-time in clarifying the issues—especially in the science tasks *Work and Energy* and *Spaceman*—yet they were still left with problems of clarification. Here is the beginning of Group 4's attempt at *Work and Energy*:

1. Bill: There's no work involved in electricity to light a light bulb.

2. Jeanette: No I don't think so.

3. Bill: Unless, erm, unless you, erm, involve the work of the men in the turbine station that produces the electricity to make the light.

The *Work and Energy* task with its tight definitions of those two concepts might at first glance seem to leave the group with nothing to do but to apply these definitions to the given examples. But no task can be as clear as that, for the definitions themselves have to be interpreted. In this example, Bill seems to be facing two problems as he tries to use the teacher's conceptual scheme as a tool of thinking:

1. separating the technical meaning of "work" from the everyday concept ("the work of the men in the turbine station")
2. determining the limits of the given example ("Electricity to light a light bulb"), that is, whether it includes the generation of the electricity.

The first of these is a familiar problem in science teaching; it is noteworthy that Bill is still not clear about "work" in spite of the discussion in the lesson. The second was quite unexpected, for the teacher and researchers had taken this boundary as self-evident. However clearly the teacher frames an exposition or chooses questions, the learner must use what she knows already in order to make sense of them. In the groups we are able to observe this happening; in lessons which restrict opportunities for learners to speak it must go on silently, if at all.

The construction of the question is a different matter in non-scientific topics such as *Causes of Vandalism* and *The Pearl*. Neither the boundaries of the task nor the concepts to be used have been sharply defined. The pupils are not faced with the problem of projecting themselves into the teacher's conceptual scheme; instead they must construct one for themselves. In these cases, the construction of questions may form the predominant part of the discussion and be indistinguishable from the construction of answers. Since the progressive definition of the problem—or problems—goes on throughout the discussion it is diffuse and therefore difficult to illustrate, but two sections from the beginning of Group 2's *The Pearl* discussion will give some impression. It will be remembered that the task gave students a very open brief to discuss good and evil in the story. They begin thus:

2. Audrey: In, in this book I think it's trying to get through to you that money, is evil, and when you possess money you tend, you tend to, to take, to take it for granted and then, buy things and spend it.

3. Sylvia: Spend it on anything that you just fancy, that's in fashion, probably, what we do.

Out of the many moral issues which they might have chosen they have in fact gone to one of the novel's major themes, though here they state it in terms of their own experience. As they develop the theme, however, it becomes more closely focused upon the issues which are presented in the novel.

13. Sylvia: And you probably think that what Kino's spending when he gets that, when he sells the pearl and gets money for that we'll probably think, you know, getting married, spending the money on getting married when they're already, living together and that. . . .

Relates the idea of self-indulgent spending to the novel, not in terms of what *would happen* but as a hypothetical reader's response to the events.

14. Arthur: They, they—all the people round table, they says that, er, they'd spend it on charities but Kino and his wife says they're going to spend it on, erm, on themselves.

Focuses the issue of appropriate spending by using an episode in the novel.

15. Sylvia: Yes.

16. Paul: I bet, I bet they'd all spend it on themselves. I mean, I bet they wouldn't spend it on charities and all that, they'd spend it on themselves.

Questions whether Kino's neighbors, "the people round the table," would in real life do what they advise Kino to do—which is an appropriate interpretation of that episode.

17. Sylvia: I wouldn't spend it on charities.

18. Audrey: I know I wouldn't. . . . I mean, the people in the village know that Kino and his wife are going to spend it silly, and not give it to worthwhile causes.

Relating novel to their own motives. Takes the interpretation of the episode one step further.

What seems to be happening in the whole episode—both before and after this extract—is that the group members are sharpening their focus upon two parallel issues. One is the question of what is a morally defensible way of spending a large windfall of money. The other is how to interpret the behavior and attitudes of "all the people round the table," that is the neighbors who speak of what they would do if they had found the pearl.

In describing this kind of discussion as *constructing questions* we do not mean that the young people necessarily formulate them as questions—though sometimes they do, as we have shown. It is rather that a discussion of this more open kind is made up of a series of attempts to arrive at a shared framework such that after a while some contributions will seem relevant, and others will seem irrelevant or changes of subject. This building up of a framework of relevance is more obviously present in more open discussions, but is nevertheless going on in all of them. In some of the topics, such as *Work and Energy*, they construct this framework with half an eye on their teacher's intentions, and are attempting to conform to what they believe to be his view of what is relevant.

Raising New Questions

It was in the nature of this study that in designing the task we should follow the wishes of the teachers we were collaborating with. This has meant that in some tasks the attention of the pupils was tightly structured by a series of questions and that in others they were more free to find issues for themselves. This section illustrates the way in which our thirteen-year-olds are able to move outside the given framework and ask useful questions of their own, all three of the examples being taken from discussions of the *Spaceman* topic where the tightly-framed set questions make it easy to recognize when the pupils raise issues of their own.

The three boys in Group 16 had given a very competent explanation of why the cork was expelled from the bottle when the pressure outside it had been lowered. Then suddenly, in the midst of this discussion, one of them considered as a hypothetical possibility the reversal of the relative pressure so that the pressure was greater outside the bottle.

29. Philip: If it had been put the other way round it would have, it would have. . . .   Raises new possibility. (Interrupted)

30. Edward: Well it was, it was wasn't it?

Misunderstanding?

31. Philip: No I mean if. . . .

Attempts to explain.

32. Harold: Yes.

Supports Edward.

33. Philip: No, I mean if there was air on the outside, and not in the bottle it would just. . . .

Expands his own earlier contribution (No. 29).

34. Edward: Nothing would have happened.

Dismisses the hypothetical case.

35. Philip: It would.

36. Harold: It would cave in, wouldn't it?

Harold now sees the point.

37. Philip: It would cave in. Because if there's no pressure on the bottle.

Attempts to justify his assertion.

38. Harold: It would crush it, wouldn't it?

Completes Philip's explanation.

39. Philip: . . . no pressure forcing out of the bottle. . . . (and so on)

Rephrases.

The two boys, Harold and Philip, have explored this counter-possibility, and Edward joins in later. In the preceding exchanges Edward had dominated the discussion: this may explain his initial failure to understand Philip's suggestion and his attempt to dismiss it. The egocentric desire to display knowledge is frequently in effective opposition to the wish to collaborate in constructing knowledge. The alternative case which Philip has put forward has given the group a useful opportunity to test their grasp of the underlying principle. The task, however, had not suggested to them that they should try other possible cases.

To take another example, when the boys of Group 15 discuss the final question of the *Spaceman* task (that is, what would happen to a man if he went outside a space ship without a space suit), members of the group raise a series of new topics. They have agreed that the man would explode, and Barry asks: "How does a space suit stop it? Is there air inside?" A few moments later Barry compares a space suit to a diving suit, and then asks: "I wonder how fish and all them survive down there then." Later they discuss why flat fish are flat. They are able to extrapolate from what they have learnt, and indeed are eager to integrate and interrelate this with a wide range of knowledge which they already have. In comparison, the given topic, in its attempt to encourage explicit explanation and a thorough grasp of the principles involved, fails to ask for some relevant understanding which these boys possess.

The girls of Group 12, although they approach the *Spaceman* questions systematically and with serious intentions, display some lack of grasp of the concept of pressure when they are working within the framework given to them. But one of them is able to criticize the assumptions upon which one of the questions is based, the question which asks, *If a piece of rock hit a spaceship and made a hole in it, what would happen to the air inside?*

30. Nicola: Also if a spaceship is up in the, you know, up in the air, up in the, you know, space and there's no air around and the rock is floating about, the rock down, down, you know, you know, on the land level would be heavy.

31. Teresa: Yes.

32. Nicola: But up, you know, past gravity and that....

33. Teresa: Yes, it's light as a sponge.

34. Nicola: It'll be, it'll be, it'll be, it'll be light as a sponge. So I think that's really a daft question because I don't think a rock in space could, you know, force a hole in a spaceship.

Nicola has misinterpreted statements about the *weightlessness* of objects in a moving spaceship to imply that at a distance from the earth objects are "past gravity" (i.e., beyond the reach of gravity), and therefore have no mass. This idea she transfers to a piece of rock coming from elsewhere, deducting that it will be "light as a sponge" and that it therefore will lack the momentum to pierce the metal skin of a spaceship. Within the bounds of her current understanding of the phenomena, Nicola is reasoning with commendable ingenuity and consistency and making a useful effort to relate the set question to her understanding of the behavior of masses in space. Her criticism of the question is a mark of her awareness that the two do not match. Unfortunately they do not pursue this issue further.

A similar flexibility in raising new questions was shown in the discussion based on other topics, and especially by Groups 1 to 4, who became more experienced at working in groups. Both *The Pearl* and *National Parks* in their very nature required the students to select their own frames of reference, and their ability to do so has already been illustrated in the section in Chapter 2 concerned with *initiating moves*. The tightly structured series of questions used in certain topics probably helped the groups achieve concentration and clarity but may have impeded them from relating the new knowledge to what they already knew. For teaching purposes there might have been some value in appending to the set questions an invitation to raise doubts, pursue new examples, suggest new issues and so on.

Setting Up Hypotheses

In the nature of things most of the contributions put forward by members of the groups were hypothetical, at least in the sense that they involved going beyond the given information in setting up an explanation or an interpretation. A convenient example comes from the end of Group 4's discussion of *The Pearl*.

123. Pauline: I wonder what made him write such a story.

124. Bill: Probably, erm, thought that the plight of these sort of people was worth writing about so that they'd, erm, so that everybody would know what it was like to live in a village and feel a bit sorry for them, you know.

The deliberate attempt to build an explanation out of hints and impressions leads them towards a valuable insight.

What we are concerned with here, however, are explicit hypotheses, where a student sets up an alternative possibility in order to explore how it would work. These often arose as implicit ways of testing the generality of explanations used to account for the given case, but not always. Our first example is a simple one. Alan begins Group 4's discussion of *Steve's Letter* with the hesitant assertion, "I don't think you'd write that to your best mate or your friend would you?", but a few speeches later Pauline retorts:

7. Pauline: Yes, but he might not be a best friend.

8. Alan: Eh no, just, just say if it was. . . . (and so on)

Pauline is perfectly right to doubt whether Steve's employer is likely to be his best friend, yet Alan has a good reason for insisting that the implications of that possibility should be explored, since a moment later he reaches the important insight that an appropriate style would depend on the person addressed. (This may seem obvious to the reader, but it was not in the least obvious to these thirteen-year-olds.) The next two contributions ran in fact in this way:

9. Pauline: Well it's his boss, isn't it?

10. Alan: He, he'd put different things, wouldn't he? It depends who he's writing to really.

Thus, this minor—and apparently unrealistic—hypothesis led to a significant contribution to the discussion.

We have already seen how Group 16 tested its explanation of why the cork was ejected from the bottle by considering what would have happened had the bottle been made of plastic, of thin or thick glass, and then by discussing what would have happened had the greater pressure been outside, instead of inside, the bottle. This testing against hypothetical cases did not seem to be a deliberate technique, but to be put forward piecemeal by members of the group as they thought of cases which it would be interesting to consider.

The importance of the strategy *setting up hypotheses* is that it invites the group to test the hypothesis by relating it to other information and to explanatory models that they have available. In discussing these relationships, the students will be carrying out precisely those processes of monitoring and re-shaping understanding that are at the center of learning.

Using Evidence

In any learning the learners have to utilize what they already know in order to give meaning to new insights or information which they are given. New understanding is likely to be a reorganization of old knowledge rather than solely an addition to it. Thus, an essential cognitive strategy is the ability to utilize previous knowledge and experience to throw light upon the matter in hand. This section is concerned both generally with the students' use of their existing knowledge as a resource and with their more explicit use of information in the testing of assertions.

It was the two tasks relating to violence among adolescent boys that most obviously invited the groups to utilize their everyday knowledge. Group 9 began their *Gang Violence* discussion with:

Catherine: Well if you remember when we went to London, Elizabeth, when, you know, in the tube [subway] station (Yes) there were lots, we saw people with bottles and that, and knives, that's because there's a football match on and I suppose this is the difference because, one supports one team and one supports another and if you remember. . . . (and so on)

Such direct use of first-hand anecdote was infrequent, however, and may only have occurred here because Catherine and Elizabeth are sisters. More commonly in the *Gang Violence* and *Causes of Vandalism* topics the students used their first-hand knowledge— which in some cases seemed extensive—to build up typical cases of violence or to characterize imaginary gang members and their motives. Here is Group 4 (*Causes of Vandalism*):

17. Alan: They've nothing to do so they say, "Come on we'll stir up a bit of trouble."

18. Bill: Yes, it starts off as a bit of fun, you know, sort of a pretend fight.

19. Alan: It starts off with their fists and somebody gets rough.

20. Bill: Yes.

21. Alan: And somebody uses a bottle or chains or hammers, something like that.

22. Pauline: Yes.

23. Jeanette: Yes, and they do it for no reason at all.

24. Bill: Well it depends doesn't it. . . . (and so on)

Their strategy for discussing the cause of violence is to utilize their background knowledge to construct a hypothetical case which can thereafter be used as a basis for explicit generalization. The hypothetical case itself is an implicit generalization; although it is made up of concrete details, these are implicitly held to be general. This can be seen as a special case of the strategy described above as *constructing the question*: it is as if the group had found the interview with the gang leader, Ron, to be an inadequate basis for a discussion of motives and had therefore supplied far more data in the form of typical cases. On the basis of this data they can then go on to deal explicitly with the question of motives: Jeanette in the extract above makes an explicit generalization, "They do it for no reason at all," which provokes Bill to question the generality of her statement:

24. Bill: Well it depends doesn't it. There may be two or three gangs going around and if somebody wants to, there may be just one discotheque and with two or three gangs it gets a bit crowded so everybody loses their temper and then it starts off with fists and then turns into a full-scale rumble, a fight and that.

Bill is questioning the generality of Jeanette's statement not by another explicit generalization but by putting forward another and different typical case, which is itself an implicit generalization. It is important to notice that although much of the discussion of these two topics is conducted in all the groups through hypothetical cases, this does not mean that these thirteen-year-olds are incapable of generalized thinking about social issues. Indeed, their hypothetical cases, which might at a glance be dismissed as low-level *concrete* thinking, function as generalizations. The use of an example is certainly not blocking them off from access to contradictory examples or—as Bill shows—from awareness of the general principles implicit in the examples.

It is not only in the more open topics that the groups utilize knowledge from everyday life. In *Work and Energy* it is not possible to apply the definitions of *work* and *energy* to examples without using everyday knowledge about steam engines, light bulbs, and so on. Bill is once again particularly successful in linking school concepts with his everyday knowledge:

29. Bill: Although you could, erm, connect something to the steam engine, so you could have heat to movement in the steam engine, the steam engine connected by pulley to a turbine, producing electricity to light a light bulb.

This witty display of how the two examples of change in form of energy given in the task could be joined by a string of changes is exceptional. Links between the tasks and everyday life were made by all groups: indeed the questions could hardly be discussed without using knowledge of how things are in the world.

So far *evidence* has been used loosely to refer to the bringing in of knowledge from outside the school. Yet thirteen-year-olds are capable of using evidence in the stricter sense, that is, of deliberately adducing arguments to support or disprove a general assertion. We have already quoted the end of Group 1's discussion of the verisimilitude of Steinbeck's *The Pearl* and now turn for our example to the beginning of that episode.

34. David: Well I, the best part I liked were, when, when he went looking for the pearl down in the sea, did you?

Initiates new focus with expression of approval.

35. Marianne: Yes it should have des, —had a bit more description about the actual diving.

Accepts the focus but qualifies the approval with a criticism.

36. Barbara: Yes, of the sea.

Offers an alternative version of the criticism.

37. David: Yes.

38. Marianne: Because, if, if he's supposed to be a diver he hadn't spent much time, diving has he?

Offers evidence to support the general assertion.

39. David: He just went down and it was there waiting for him, wasn't it?

Extending Marianne's contribution, adding further evidence.

40. Marianne: He should have had to search for it first.

Further extending.

41. Barbara: It seems a bit funny that as soon as baby gets hurt....

Offers different evidence to support Marianne's assertion.

42. Marianne: That he should find the pearl.

Completes Barbara's contribution.

In this exchange, Group 1 members without any prompting turn to their memories of the text to find supporting evidence, since it is clear that all three have at one point or another found this part of the novel unrealistic (as it is intended to be). Such references to incidents of the novel were common in several groups' discussions of *The Pearl*. We have already illustrated several occasions when a sceptical student has asked another for supporting evidence, for example Louise's "What makes you think so?" in Group 5's *Bird's Eggs* which we quoted as an example of *eliciting*. Whereas for the most part the bringing forward of evidence to support or challenge assertions is done by normal *extending* or *qualifying* moves, there are occasions when the group members quite explicitly ask for evidence or supply it. Although for the most part the construction of knowledge is carried on intuitively, without reflection, when necessary the production of evidence can represent a deliberate and conscious strategy. This theme of reflective and conscious strategies will be developed later.

Expressing Feelings and Recreating Experience

Not all of the topics discussed in the groups were so separate from what mattered in the young people's lives that they could withdraw from commitment and discuss them with the detachment which (perhaps wrongly) is often held to be *academic*. Some topics came close enough to a student's own concerns to call forth expressions of feeling. These should be distinguished from the expressions of feeling towards one another which were as likely to be generated during neutral topics as during those concerned with urgent issues. With the expression of feeling about the topic we are linking the recreation of remembered responses to literature, since it is a characteristic of a good story to strike a spark of sympathetic feeling in the reader, even when the events of the story are concerned with people distant from the student's experience.

One might have expected the *Causes of Vandalism* topics to generate feelings, but those were on the whole treated as something that happened to someone else, even though these persons were often claimed as acquaintances. Expressions of feeling occurred frequently during the discussion of *Life in the Trenches*, a task which we have not had occasion to mention before. In previous lessons a teacher had presented to the class a variety of information about the First World War. This had included a film and examples of letters and publications of the period. Besides this, the pupils were probably able to call on other information from television programs and elsewhere. The task required the pupils to discuss life in the trenches during the war, stressing the soldiers' experience of danger and discomfort. A few exchanges from Group 7 can represent many of the expressions of feeling generated by what they had seen and heard.

94. Mary: And so many people get killed a day don't they, quite a lot of people? Yes.

95. Dorothy: Yes and if, if I were there, erm. . . .

96. Gordon: Oh I don't know.

97. Dorothy: I'd hate it if any of me good pals got killed or anything.

98. Gordon: Got killed.

99. Mary: Yes, I know.

100. Dorothy: It's horrible, you see them dying on the picture though.

101. Mary: Mm.

The common feeling generated in the group is patent even in transcription, and it is clearly most relevant to the topic which they are discussing.

It would have been difficult to predict, however, what one boy said during such a discussion in Group 6:

12. Carl: It was daft wasn't it?

13. Paula: What was?

14. Carl: The First World War.

15. Paula: What d'you mean it was daft?

16. Trevor: All bloody wars are daft aren't they?

Whatever Carl's original remark meant it gave Trevor an opportunity to express with some force what we would interpret as a general judgment. These thirteen-year-olds live in a moral world, part of which they have clearly mapped so that they can make certain moral judgments with clarity and warmth. It might perhaps be added that Trevor's contribution shows yet another form of knowledge which may be brought into school, an ethical principle very different from the particular cases discussed above under the heading *Using Evidence*.

   In the previous section we showed Group 1 criticizing parts of *The Pearl* for a lack of verisimilitude. This criticism did not, however, negate their very real appreciation of the novel. Marianne had asked for more description of "the actual diving," and in reply David reminds the group of part of the diving which had been told in detail. (Part of this was quoted in Chapter 2 for another purpose).

59. David: Well when he came. . . . Well they described that how long he held his breath. When, when he came up and when he, when he slipped a knife into it [i.e. the oyster], it tightened up and he couldn't open it.

60. Marianne: Mm, that was good.

61. David: And when, when he did eventually open it, er, he said, the pearl were as big as, erm. . . .

62. Marianne: As his hand. It just laid in his hand, didn't it?

Rehearsing the incident has recreated for these two their own remembered enjoyment in reading the episode. Marianne's tone as she says, "As his hand. It just laid in his hand, didn't it?" expresses the relish she feels at the image of the enormous pearl. Such recreation of response to the story was not uncommon in the discussions of *The Pearl*, though the explicit "Mm, that was good" might be difficult to match from another group.

   It is important not to restrict *the construction of knowledge* so that it applies only to knowledge distant from the knower's own concerns, since our most important knowledge is not of that kind. The knowledge which bears directly on the students' daily lives, and on which they base their actions, has its own important part to play in school learning.

Reflexivity

As we have seen, the adolescents in our sixteen groups collaborated in sequential and meaningful talk, managed their social relationships, and adopted rational strategies in coping with the tasks. But how far were they aware of doing all these things? How far could they monitor their own behavior so as to adjust and modify their strategies? Piaget's studies of young people's cognitive development had led us to expect that our average thirteen-year-olds, given familiar subject matter and helpful circumstances, would be reaching out towards the more reflective forms of thought which characterize what Piaget called the formal operational stage of development. One would expect them to be able occasionally to see their own viewpoint as one among several possible ones and to relate within overarching principles their own and other people's viewpoints; to be able to set up hypothetical explanations and to test them; to be able to evaluate their own and others' viewpoints, treating them as open to modification; and to be consciously choosing the cognitive strategies used and some of the social skills. We have already illustrated some of these characteristics of hypothetico-deductive thinking; here we are particularly concerned with self-awareness and the occasions when the students explicitly monitored their own strategies. Since they depend upon the learners' ability to reflect upon their thinking, we deal with these characteristics together here under the heading of *reflexivity*.

In this section we consider the monitoring by the young people of their own speech and thought strategies, their ability to interrelate alternative viewpoints, their evaluating of their own and others' performances, and their awareness of the group's strategies. Finally, we note that there are circumstances under which reflexivity is not necessary.

Monitoring Their Thinking

We begin with some examples which show at a very simple level that a student is listening to what he or she is saying and evaluating it. This becomes clear when Alec in Group 15, for example, corrects himself in mid-sentence, aware that what he is saying will be understood in ways that do not match his intentions. He is explaining why the cork comes out in the *Spaceman* task when he realizes that he has not said what he intended:

8. Alec: There's an even pressure on the bottle which let, keeps the cork on.

He seems to have begun to say that equal pressure inside and outside the bottle would "let" the cork stay in place and then to have realized that this carries unwanted associations of giving permission to a human being, so that he hastily substitutes "keeps."

A more important kind of self-awareness is shown by Bill when members of Group 4 are talking about water in their *Work and Energy* discussion:

20. Alan: It moves downstream and it, it turns, turbines to make electricity and it can use it to be a water mill as well.	Applying the concept of change of energy to the movement of water downhill.
21. Bill: That could be a follow on, you could say, erm, water to tur-	Attempts a systematic analysis of the changes in energy linking falling water to the generation of light.

bine, turbine to, to, erm, energy, energy to electricity to light in a light bulb.	
You could say that, couldn't you?	Checks that Alan would accept this formulation.

Here we interpret the repeated phrase "could say" as showing that Bill regards his analytical account not as absolute but as an interpretation open to later modification. That is, he is aware of taking part in the construction of knowledge, and—appropriately—regards that knowledge as provisional. We have already quoted (in the section *using evidence*) an occasion from the *Causes of Vandalism* discussion in which Bill uses the phrase "Well, it depends, doesn't it?" to indicate that he wishes two alternative accounts to be considered together: this seems to show an analogous pattern of thought.

Many of the examples put forward in the last section under the headings of *Raising New Questions* and *Setting Up Hypotheses* depend equally on the ability to hold simultaneously several alternative possibilities and to follow their implications. This can also be linked with the more self-conscious demands for evidence, such as David's "Well where's the force?" in Group 1's discussion of *Work and Energy*. Such awareness of evidence provides the students with a method for evaluating the alternative possibilities.

Relating Alternative Constructions

The ability to treat viewpoints as hypothetical carries with it the possibility of according validity to others' views even when they clash with one's own. The following may be primarily a tactful gesture which we might have used in the section on social skills to illustrate how one of the girls is able to soften her disagreement by acknowledging the validity of expressing the opinion she is contradicting. On the other hand it could equally be an acknowledgment that the other's suggestion makes sense in its own terms. Group 4 is discussing whether buildings such as restaurants should be allowed in national parks. One of the boys thinks that such buildings, if surrounded by trees, would be acceptable.

18. Alan: Yes, but I think you could have all these buildings, if they were specially camouflaged. Say you build your restaurants, and you have them opened—and your front, with the front on to the road and trees surrounding it.

19. Pauline: Yes but even that. . . .

20. Alan: You know, big trees so you wouldn't be able to see it, you know, so it would not, wouldn't spoil the view.

21. Jeanette: Yes, you could look at it like that. I think these things that are in towns, like nightclubs and casinos are going to spoil it.

It is not easy to determine the meaning of Jeanette's "You could look at it like that." It is certainly of social value in ensuring that the contrary view she is about to express does not destroy the group's sense of a common direction. At the same time, it seems to be an acknowledgment that Alan's argument about concealing the buildings is persuasive: here the cognitive and the social go hand in hand.

In Group 1 Marianne provides rather different evidence of using the deliberate strategy of holding more than one viewpoint in mind during the discussion. In their *National Parks* discussion David reminds the group of the claims of those visitors who come to the parks for walking.

4. David: I think the people who, er, do a lot of walking have got more right to it than, er, you know, the machines have, the cars and buses and things.

5. Marianne: Yes, well we'll have to consider their point of view as well.

As with the previous example, Marianne's reply can be seen as a tactful move to avoid a head-on clash between members of the group who are stressing the needs of walkers and those who are stressing the needs of motorists. However, it is also a necessary cognitive strategy, for the *National Parks* topic is analogous to a committee issue; any reasonable discussion would involve mediation between the conflicting interests of hikers, motorists and local communities. For this purpose, Marianne is making a valuable *chairperson's move* in explicitly acknowledging conflicting points of view.

As we have already seen in Group 4's *Work and Energy* discussion, when Bill is compelled to answer the set question *Is work always done when energies change in form?* he parries this with "No not always. It depends what you'd classify as work." Bill, like other students in the groups, was having difficulty in using the given definition of *work* ("Work is done when a force moves") and was finding it easier to use everyday versions of the concept.

The phrase "It depends. . . ." can be interpreted in two ways. Bill may be showing himself to be aware that he is moving between different definitions and that these must affect his reply to the question. On the other hand the strategy may be habitual: it is difficult to tell when an habitual phrase becomes a strategy of thought. His physics teacher would probably not approve of his strategy; our interest, however, lies in noticing his nascent awareness of what he is doing.

On another occasion Bill uses a similar method to deal with a difference of opinion. Group 4 is talking about the social context in which the story of *The Pearl* is set.

61. Bill: . . . .around that age when everybody was sort of primitive in that area.

62. Alan: Not so primitive really because. . . .

63. Bill: Well?

64. Alan: If you look at the doctor, he had, he had chocolate and he had guards and that, didn't he really? Servants.

65. Bill: Well, primitive in the way that people didn't have tractors and ploughs and sort of. . . .

From one point of view Bill is defending himself from Alan's contrary argument, but underlying this seems to be the realization that they are disagreeing because they are using different definitions of "primitive." It is an important cognitive ability to see one's own and others' knowledge as constructs which depend upon underlying assumptions, which are often unstated. From time to time, throughout Group 4's discussion, Alan and Bill identify differences of assumption which underlie surface clashes of opinion.

Such awareness of alternative constructions is important not for its own sake but as a step towards finding a framework in which both are meaningful. This does not mean reconciling them: the framework may supply grounds for understanding why the two viewpoints are irreconcilably different. It will be remembered that Alan contributed to the discussion of *Steve's Letter* the idea that an appropriate style depends on the writer's relationship with the recipient: "It depends who he's writing to really." However, the members of the group continued to express contrary views, some wishing Steve to express violent dissatisfaction in order to satisfy his indignation, while others wished him to write "respectfully," as to an older man. It was not until much later in the discussion that Group 4 began to find a framework which made sense of both these points of view, after having returned several times to this issue:

160. Bill: You want to tell him you didn't really enjoy it but then again you don't want to tell him, you don't want to be, erm, sort of, left out in the cold next year so you haven't got, er, a job.

Bill seems to be on the edge of grasping that the letter needs to be polite enough not to break off communication, but strong enough to make it clear that Steve would not accept the job again without better working conditions.

We found that our groups commonly returned several times to unsolved issues. Each time the issue was tacitly abandoned, but after a while it was introduced again, often with added insight gained from the intervening discussion of related matters. It seems likely that this cyclic pattern is typical of informal discussions.

In the last two cases quoted, the acknowledgment that others' points of view are valid goes far beyond being a skillful gesture of social tact. Bill is seeking a relationship between the two viewpoints, an overarching principle which will contain both of them. This is indeed an important ability which underlies a wide range of higher-level cognitive skills.

Evaluating

It should not be thought that the groups were always concerned about achieving consensus, that they always avoided evaluating their own or others' contributions, or the overall achievement of the group. We have already looked at clashes of opinion: our concern here is those points at which evaluation is made explicit.

Under the heading *supportive behavior* in the previous chapter we quoted examples from Group 1 and Group 4 of their ability to encourage one another. Bill says "Yes, that a, that's a good idea," to Pauline, and David, in expressing his enjoyment of *The Pearl* and his satisfaction at what their discussion had achieved, twice uses the same exclamation, "Super." These episodes were used there to illustrate the young people's social skills, but they can also be considered as examples of reflexivity. Part of these two groups' success in discussion seemed to lie in their ability occasionally to step outside their own constructing of knowledge and make that the object of their attention. It should not, however, be concluded that such moves were common even in Groups 1 and 4. For example, only on one occasion during the *Work and Energy* discussions did one member of a group praise another's contribution, and this occurred in Group 4. It will be remembered that Bill constructed an ingenious series of changes in the form of energy so as to link a steam engine to an electric light bulb. Our attention here will be directed towards Pauline's response to this.

29. Bill: Although you could, erm, connect something to the steam engine so you could have heat to movement in the steam engine, the steam engine connected by pulley to a turbine, producing electricity to light a bulb.

30. Jeanette: Mm, mm, yes, yes.

31. Pauline: Hey, that's good is that.

Pauline's remark seems to be an immediate expression of admiration of Bill's ingenuity, but also to mark a sudden insight into the possibility of infinite strings of changes in the form of energy. How far she is aware of the nature of this insight is, of course, another matter. This kind of explicit recognition of the appropriateness or ingenuity of a contribution is, however, relatively rare in the discussions.

It is not difficult to find occasions when members of the groups make sharply dismissive remarks about others' contributions; these often seem to indicate an awareness that the discussion is not going well. The two girls who attempted the *Carbon Dioxide in Water* task—Christine and Margaret of Group 3—found themselves immediately in disagreement. They had been asked to explain why the apparatus only let air in by one tube and only let air out through the other.

4. Margaret: Oh, well. Because that one's a long one, because that one's a long one and that one's a little one. And it goes in through the long one then out of the little one. No, it goes in through the long one. . . .

5. Christine: You don't know what you're talking about.

6. Margaret: No, no.

7. Christine: No you see, there's a little stopper, and it's got two holes in.

8. Margaret: I know, I said that.

9. Christine: You didn't.

10. Margaret: No I didn't say that, but I meant that.

Christine's judgment that Margaret doesn't know what she is talking about, though perhaps justified, takes the thinking no further. It operates merely as a means of silencing Margaret so that Christine can take the floor, as in fact she does at the next utterance, No. 11. (It is relevant to note that when these girls take part in Group 3's discussions they are frequently aggressive to one another.) In this case the negative evaluation seems to have contributed nothing to the ensuing construction of knowledge: it acts as a dismissal of Margaret as well as her contribution. When a qualifying move follows an inadequate contribution, it can reinforce what is valid in what has been said, and by modifying the line of thought, offer a profitable direction to the discussion. We have not found in the discussions any occasions when an explicit negative judgment seems to have helped the group towards better thinking: expressions of alternative opinion which do not damage the group members' self-respect seemed more valuable.

Awareness of Strategies

We would not expect thirteen-year-olds to plan an agenda for themselves, and few groups in fact did so. Where detailed questions were given most groups followed these in the given order, though Group 12 inexplicably began the *Spaceman* task with the final question.

1. Nicola: Right, are we doing number four? Have we to do number four first?

2. Teresa: Read it out (whispered). Read it out.

3. Nicola: No, why?

4. Teresa: They know what the question is.

5. Sheila: Well they'll already know.

6. Nicola: Oh, yes, well I know what. If we read the little introduction bit they'll know what we're on about, about, what, we're on about.

7. Teresa: Yes, then we can all discuss after it then.

Group 12 members show themselves unusually aware of the future audience for their recording and are well able to plan for its needs, making deliberate choices of the order in which they answered the questions.

   Where no sequence of questions had been provided all groups set off on a topic chosen at random. This proved to be an appropriate strategy. It would only be possible to set up an agenda on the basis of an existing sense of which issues were relevant, and which had priority of importance; the whole purpose of topics such as *The Pearl* and *Gang Violence* was that through talk the groups should shape such a sense of relevance and priority. To set up an agenda they would need already to have partly achieved this. Although the discussion was often circular, returning to a topic several times, there was often a perceptible improvement in the group's grasp of the issue when they returned. For example, Group 4 in discussing *Steve's Letter* returned again and again to the disagreement about whether it should frankly express Steve's feelings or be framed in a respectful tone.

   We have already discussed under the heading of *social skills* in Chapter 2 the means by which the groups controlled their progress through the tasks and determined the boundaries of what was relevant. Much of this was carried out implicitly, through the give and take of eliciting and responding moves of various kinds. Where choices were made explicitly, this could equally have been discussed here as an example of reflexivity. The examples used in the last chapter to discuss how groups negotiate an agreement about when their task is completed would also have been applicable here.

Summarizing

One means by which a group can monitor its progress through a discussion, and check upon points of agreement and disagreement, is through summarizing. A person who offers a summary is often for the moment detaching him or herself from the give and take of the group: such *chairperson's moves* may be potentially threatening to a group's sense of a common purpose since the temporary chairperson may seem to be claiming authority. The presence of the tape recorder on several occasions gave a reason for a summarizing move, though as we have seen in Group 15, Barry's "We've now done two, Tape," is part of an attempt to make the running which is soon challenged by the others. Jeanette's easy summary of Bill's long description of the doctor in *The Pearl*, "Money grabbing, you mean?" is much less threatening, because she is clearly doing so in order to confirm that she has understood. But this is not the kind of summary which we are referring to. What is particularly valuable is the summary which is itself a major contribution to the constructing of knowledge, putting together in one statement a number of viewpoints which had been offered separately.

A form of summarizing is used occasionally to close off an episode in preparation for moving to another topic. Most changes of topic are carried out either implicitly in the course of a series of expansion moves or through an initiating move which redirects the discussion after a pause. In one or two cases, however, the initiating move is preceded by a brief summary. Here Group 1, talking about *The Pearl*, has put forward several episodes which seem to them to lack verisimilitude, and Barbara is returning yet again to one of these.

85. Barbara: I think he should describe more, you know. It's supposed to be about diving and pearls.	Returning to previous sub-topic.
86. Marianne: Yes, we don't think, we don't think there's adequate description.	Summarising consensus already attained.
87. David: Yes, no. The doctor was a bit evil though wasn't he?	Accepts the summary. Raises a fresh topic (related to the given task).

Marianne's summary prevented a merely repetitive return to the earlier issues, and enabled David to move the discussion on.

In Group 3's discussion of *National Parks*, Robert summarizes in order to draw the group back on to the main issues when they appeared in danger of being sidetracked on to talk about swimming in lakes. (Part of this exchange has already been quoted.)

23. Robert: Yes, well the people, well most people, don't like swimming in lakes because they think they're dirty.

24. Christine: Yes, they are.

25. Robin: More warmer anyway.

26. Robert: It's more warmer, if they build swimming pools it'd be warmer, more warmer, more warmer. But really the national parks were set up to, keep them, as natural as possible but if man keeps coming in and taking over all these areas, well there isn't going to be anything left is there for anybody, any later generation?

Robert first summarizes what has been said about lakes and swimming pools, thus implicitly defining this sub-topic as completed. Then, signalling a change of sub-topic by the phrase "but really," he restates the general drift of the whole discussion so far. Then after a pause they set out on a new sub-topic.

In discussing reflexivity we have tried to keep in mind that the value of reflective thought is open to question. What we have called *reflexive* utterances were not very common in the discussions, and it is possible—and even probable—that there was much more self-awareness and reflective thought than was ever put into words. We may indeed be mistaken in putting such emphasis upon self-awareness: as we have shown, there was much good discussion in the groups that organized itself without recourse to explicit self-monitoring. This was particularly true when members of the group could confidently and briefly answer the set questions. Under these circumstances neither tentativeness nor a high level of reflexivity seemed necessary: both are perhaps most called for when a learner has to adapt a well-established pattern to thinking in order to cope with new information or with someone else's alternative pattern. Some of the reflexive utterances illustrated here may have more properly belonged among the social skills than among the cognitive abilities: some were certainly associated with the tactful recognition of other people's interests. It could be, nevertheless, that strategies adopted in the first place in order to find social solutions to differences of opinion may later be adapted as cognitive strategies for finding overarching principles which relate the two. Students' ability to take part in social negotiation and their ability to take account of others' viewpoints probably develop together: it would not seem profitable to name one as cause and the other as effect.

Most of our examples of reflexivity have come from a relatively limited number of students. About a third of those quoted came from Bill of Group 4, though the others are spread across different groups. Some members of the groups proved to be capable of reflexive awareness of their own and others' thinking, and this appears to have contributed to the quality of some of the discussions.

Analyzing the Data

Throughout this chapter and the previous one we have used a descriptive system we developed as a result of analyzing our data. This system distinguished between social and cognitive functions of learning conversations among small groups of peers. We found this distinction helped us better to understand and illustrate the variety of complex initiatives being undertaken by the groups even though both of these functions developed at the same time and often through the means of the same utterances.

As a summary we set out the descriptive system below in Figure 3–1. Always remembering that in practice these moves or strategies often go on at the same time, the table shows all the different categories we have illustrated in Chapters 2 and 3.

We said at the beginning of Chapter 2 that we did not see the comments we put forward as the only correct interpretation of the extracts we quoted. We have also noted, from time to time, some of the false starts we made in developing an analytical scheme for the data. The problems we encountered in attempting to set up a category system will be familiar to anyone who has worked on tapes and transcripts of talk produced in informal situations. The rules for shaping interaction in our groups were very much open to negotiation.

We do not mean that there were no constraints upon them. In some ways, despite the presence of the tape recorder, we feel the students' talk we documented is closer to conversations where people talk for their own purposes than it is to classroom talk, where the teachers' purposes provide the dominant framework. Certainly, there is a fluid, dynamic quality to the talk in these discussions. And although this structural complexity makes the talk delightful to listen to, these same fluid and dynamic features also make it inappropriate to pin the talk down into a category system.

Despite its imperfections, the analytical scheme we used for these data will have served its purpose if it has begun to demonstrate to our readers the relationships we found between small scale aspects of communication in these small groups and the cognitive strategies that were constructed in the course of their dialogue. We hope that the analyses we have put forward capture something of the interplay between participation in dialogic conversations and the development of new meanings. Some of our readers will themselves wish to study talk in small learning groups and with their interests in mind we will explore issues in studying group talk in further detail in Chapter 5. However, for many readers the primary issues raised by this discussion of our materials in Chapter 2 and 3

Figure 3–1 Social and Cognitive Functions of Learning Conversations

Level One

	Initiating	Extending	Eliciting	Responding
Discourse Moves		Qualifying Contradicting	Continue Expand Bring in Support Request information	Accepting

Logical Process
- Proposes a cause
- Proposes a result
- Expands loosely (e.g. descriptive details)
- Applies a principle to a case
- Categorises
- States conditions under which statement it is valid or invalid
- Advances evidence
- Negates
- Evaluates
- Puts alternative view
- Suggests a method
- Restates in different terms

Level Two

Social Domain
- Progress through task — Clarifying given questions; Shifting topic; Ending a discussion; Managing manipulative tasks
- Competition and conflict — Competition for the floor; Contradiction; Joking; Compelling participation
- Supportive behaviour — Explicit agreement; Naming; Reference back; Explicit approval of others; Expression of shared feeling

Cognitive Strategies
- Constructing the question — Closed tasks; Open tasks
- Raising new questions
- Setting up hypotheses — Beyond the given; Explicit hypotheses
- Using evidence — Anecdote; Hypothetical cases; Using everyday knowledge; Challenging generalities
- Expressing feelings and recreating experience — Expressing ethical judgments; Shared recreation of literary experience

Reflexivity
- Monitoring own speech and thought — Own contributions provisional
- Interrelating alternative viewpoints — Validity of others; More than one possibility; Finding overarching principles
- Evaluating own and others' performance
- Awareness of strategies — Audience for recording; Summarising; Moving to new topic

will be those related to classroom teaching. How can small group discussions be implemented in the classroom? How should a teacher set about designing appropriate tasks and what educational purposes can talk in small learning groups best achieve? How should student groups be constructed and what happens if things go wrong? We turn to these questions next in Chapter 4 which focuses on managing small group work in class.

Chapter Four

Managing Small Group
Work in Class

Many teachers use group work in one form or another, even if it is
no more than a convenient device for carrying out practical work
economically. Some teachers will say from time to time, "Discuss
it with your neighbor for a couple of minutes," while at the other
extreme some organize formal groups which work together for
weeks or months. Whatever pattern is adopted, every teacher is
likely to wonder at times whether the students are gaining as much
as possible from the work in groups, perhaps asking how best to set
them up, to structure the tasks they work on, and to establish the
form and style of his own participation. In this chapter we cannot
give simple answers to these questions. Instead, we will use our experience to suggest a range of possibilities from which teachers can
make their choices in the light of their students, their current curricular goals, and the context they are working in. We deal with the
place of group work within lessons and larger sequences, the
choice and framing of tasks, the composition of groups, the preparation of the students and support for them, and changes in the
roles required of teachers during group work.

Underlying everything we have written in this book is the idea
of the class as a context for collaborative inquiry. In the remainder
of this chapter, we explore the principles that should guide any
teacher setting up collaborative inquiry in small groups. This does
not imply that a teacher will never present material to students
through demonstration, lecture, or reading, for this is often the read-
iest way of opening up a new sequence of inquiry. However, presenting new material to the students is only the beginning of learn-

ing. Collaborative inquiry implies the introduction of a wider range of roles for both students and teacher. When a teacher sets up group discussion, it is never just a matter of using a different technique. The procedure is directed toward a different kind of learning in which the students become active agents in constructing their own understanding. It is possible to organize students into groups for the purpose of memorizing and practicing ready-made information (Slavin 1990), but this is not our topic.

As we explained in Chapter 1, in group inquiry students work upon their own understanding to make sense in their own terms of the new ideas or experiences which have been made available. This includes integrating new ideas with existing ways of thinking and understanding to modify the latter and testing where they apply and where they do not. Collaborative inquiry also includes the idea that no knowledge is final and that students need to understand this. The inquiry is collaborative in one sense because the students' efforts will at best support one another, working toward a community of understanding, and also collaborative because it requires teachers to step outside the role of academic authority in order to take part in finding out.

The social context in which group work takes place is an important determinant of its success: this is a second implication of the principle stated above that group work is not just a matter of teaching technique. For example, how the teacher normally treats students' contributions in lessons will have a marked effect upon how seriously they approach work in groups. The students whom we came to know well and who worked with us were noticeably more successful in making sense of the given tasks than others whom we met only on the day we recorded them. We conclude from this that the students' relationship with the adult who sets up group work affects their performance in the group, since this influences how they interpret the situation and their roles in it. With the former groups we had not only taken care to get to know the students, but one of their teachers had carefully explained to them that we were interested in finding out how they worked together and not in testing their speech skills. We surmise that if a teacher shows that he takes students' contributions seriously enough to reply to them rather than merely to evaluate their answers, the students are more likely to take themselves seriously when talking in small groups. That is, the teacher's behavior in lessons helps determine whether students see themselves as capable of shaping understanding.

The frequent use of small group discussion in lessons is a powerful way of showing that teachers believe in the value of talk in learning. We might then expect students who are accustomed to working together to do so with less conflict and to manage more easily the social and cognitive demands of group discussions. This happened with our groups. The students from Wickhouse School, who had had little or no experience of group work before taking part in our study, had far more difficulty in sorting out who should do what and spent more of the time competing for the opportunity to speak. It seems likely that recording itself has a considerable effect upon how students view their own talk. Recordings played back provide opportunities for students to be aware of how they think aloud and to listen to and reflect upon their own strategies. Guided reflection of this kind is an important part of successful group work, as we shall argue later when we discuss the importance of the students' understanding of learning through talk.

Introducing Students to Working in Groups

A central consideration for any teacher contemplating the setting of a task for group work is whether the students will be willing to apply themselves to it seriously enough to make the investment of time worthwhile. When the class of students is not yet familiar with small group work there is much to be said for beginning with very short collaborative activities. To take an example from social studies: before presenting material about groups living at a pre-neolithic level of technology, the teacher might ask a class of ten-year-olds to talk for a few minutes in pairs about the likely needs of human groups living in a wilderness. If this went well each pair could go on to make a list, or alternatively the teacher could list suggestions put forward by members of all the groups. The purpose of this would be to activate the students' preconceptions about the basic necessities of life in order to help them engage with the teacher's presentation: the technology and arrangements of a particular culture would thereafter be more likely to be seen not as arbitrary but as responses to universal needs. Similarly, at a later stage in the unit, when the students had achieved some understanding of the culture in question, they might again work in pairs or groups to consider ways in which the members of the culture would be likely to respond to a change in the environment—the purpose of this being both to aid the students' assimilation of the new material they had been given and to prepare for a new stage by setting up hypotheses that would eventually be confirmed or disconfirmed.

It is now that the teacher can begin to judge whether the class is ready to accept independent modes of learning. While observing from the side of the room, he can judge the level of commitment of the students to the task in hand and decide how much time should be allowed for it. At a later stage, students themselves can be asked whether they *need* more time to complete the task. Success in independent tasks on this small scale can later lead to larger groupings and longer term tasks, and perhaps eventually to work in which far more of the structure of the learning is entrusted to the learners.

Group talk is set up primarily because the teacher regards it as appropriate to particular learning that he has in mind. Preparation for this is likely to be of importance because of its effect upon the students' attitude to the topic. Nobody likes to be wrong, especially in front of rivals or superiors, so the students' sense of competence, their sense of having something relevant to contribute, will go far to determine the morale with which they approach a task and the patience with which they continue to work at it. We had no doubt that the preliminary presentation of topics in lessons played a considerable part in the success of some of the groups discussions we recorded, since the class discussion had displayed some of the approaches the students might use and shown that their ideas were taken seriously by the teacher. The very fact that the issue was presented for discussion and their suggestions responded to demonstrated that the problem could be dealt with by rational means, thus showing students that they were expected to think and not merely remember—as one of the less well-prepared groups tried to do during our second set of recordings.

In many cases the students in their groups had materials before them, printed documents or apparatus, that they could turn to for help. In lessons students turn to teachers for authoritative help; by withdrawing from directing the discussion, a teacher throws responsibility back upon the students, who must therefore make use of any available resources, both those they can retrieve from their memories and those on the table before them. If they have access to and control of apparatus or evidence such as maps, texts including facsimiles of old documents, or numerical data, this frequently lifts the quality of discussion above what could be expected if they were required to discuss abstractly.

Group Work in Longer Sequences

What we have in mind is a sequence of work that will partly be carried out under the teacher's direction and partly in smaller groups that vary in size and membership. It is useful to have in mind what sequence of activities will best contribute to students' understanding of a new area of knowledge. Reid, Forrestal, and Cook (1989)

propose five stages, which they intend as a model of an extended sequence of work within a group. However, it can equally be used as
a basis for planning a sequence of lessons, only parts of which may
be intended to take place in small groups. Their stages are:

- Engagement—refers to the provision of experience or information and includes the arousing of the students' interest.

- Exploration—is likely to be a kind of thinking aloud, an initial
  searching through the new experiences or information in relation to what the students already know and understand.

- Transformation—refers to the stage at which the teacher asks
  students to work upon the new material, for example, by clarifying, re-ordering, elaborating, and perhaps applying it to various purposes. Although Reid et al. do not say so, this seems
  likely to be the stage at which students do most to make the new
  material or way of thinking their own.

- Presentation—implies that an essential stage in group work is
  the reordering for an audience of new material produced during
  the transformation stage.

- Reflection—refers to an opportunity for the students to reflect
  explicitly both on the content of the sequence or unit of learning, and on the learning process involved in the group discussion they had experienced.

This sequence can serve as a pattern for learning activities
which would include teacher-led discussion, watching audio-visual
material, group practicals, reading, writing, and other individual
work, as well as the group discussion which is our concern here.

We have summarized this set of stages because it is valuable to
see how group discussion can play a part in a sequence of learning;
this sequence could provide the basis for planning a unit and help
teachers make systematic choices of preparatory and follow-up
work. We have already mentioned the value of the *exploration* stage
in preparing for learning, the essence of this to encourage students to
make explicit their current understanding—the basis for subsequent
learning. Equally important are the *presentation* and *reflection*
stages. However thoroughly a group of students has addressed the
task given to them, they are unlikely to have made all their thinking
explicit, even if they have been required to write down their findings
and the reasoning they can bring forward in support. Students seldom attempt of their own accord to summarize the views the group
has achieved and if required to do so will often provide only a
greatly reduced version of their discussion, with complexities and
qualifications omitted. It may be that their need for something ap-

proaching consensus leads them to turn attention away from some of the differences of opinion or policy that have divided them. For reasons such as these, it is essential for the teacher to make available opportunities for the thinking to be made explicit. Unfortunately this is often omitted, as Bennett and Dunne (1992) report.

One way to persuade students of the need for greater explicitness is by asking them to present their results to non-participants. In *presentation*, as it is recommended by Reid et al., the results are presented to a small group of peers, perhaps using a variety of the *jigsaw* method (which is described below). Presentation to a small group has the advantage of being less threatening, but we can see no reason why it should not be followed by wider presentation—to other classes, to adult visitors, or in written or display form to wider audiences. Slavin proposes a method he calls *numbered heads* for ensuring that every member of a group has the advantage of preparing for presentation: the members of each group are numbered (perhaps one to four), and when the time comes for reporting back, the teacher chooses one number at random to determine which group member should give the report. Participation in reporting is important because, once the exploratory discussion is over, the need to objectify their understanding for an audience can lay upon students a potent demand to reflect on where their thinking has led them and what precisely they do know or understand. The report stage also gives the teacher opportunities to place carefully chosen questions, to underline crucial points, to bring out evidence or arguments that have been omitted, and generally to aid students in further reordering their thoughts.

The *reflection* stage, which often follows *presentation*, has a double importance: it can lead students to a better understanding of the kind of learning they have been engaged in (Baird and Mitchell 1986) and provide the occasion for a critical reflection upon their own and other students' participation in group talk. Such self-evaluation is important partly to increase the learners' awareness of what they have achieved and what still remains, but also to enrich future collaborative study.

Reflection can sometimes gain from being done in writing, so that students clarify and make explicit to themselves what understandings they have achieved during discussion. Wells et al. (1990, 113) emphasized that writing should "form an integral component of any group learning" since it makes public "the unobservable tacit operations of the mind." This helps each student "to develop a self-conscious stance toward the completeness and coherence of his understanding." Wells also pointed out that writing allows more time for reflection and freedom from peer pressures, which may occasionally be less than helpful. However, if students perceive the writing as assessment of their achievement—which is the function of much writing in schools—this may persuade them to avoid exploring ideas in favor of the safety of *right answers*. It may even change the nature of the discussion itself: one of our groups, believing that they would be tested on a piece of writing after the discussion, became so anxious that they abandoned rational strategies and fell back upon trying to put together bits of remembered information, going over these repeatedly without advancing their understanding. It is always necessary to be aware that the setting of written work reflects different constraints upon the discussion that precedes it, according to how the students perceive the purposes of the writing.

So far we have assumed that collaborative inquiry will turn class learning into a flexible *conversation* orchestrated by the teacher, in which a whole range of activities, including reading and writing, will play a part. Small group talk will arise from the ongoing work and feed back into it, so that this talk is no more than one mode within the overall conversation. The main body of our research material was of this kind, the teachers inviting us to make recordings when their teaching had arrived at a point at which independent small group discussion seemed likely to contribute to the current work. This is not the only possibility, however. Particularly with older students and those who have shown themselves able to collaborate effectively, it is possible to set up group work in which the students manage their projects over a longer period of time. For example, older students who had completed classes in Design and Technology were given the task of designing a piece of apparatus to perform a specific function. Earlier instruction had made them aware of the need first to investigate how the apparatus was to be used and the relevant needs of likely users. They then went on to discuss and sketch out possible designs, eventually selecting two for making mock-ups or prototypes for trials. Eventually, when final choices had been made and a working version constructed, the whole sequence was written up. The sequence, which in that case lasted for many weeks, provided abundant opportunities for collaborative discussion and the sharing of tasks. Success in a long-term task of this kind rests upon previous learning, upon supported choice of appropriate tasks, and upon the teacher's unobtrusive observation, so that problems the students cannot solve can be dealt with quickly.

Choosing and Framing the Tasks

The central principle that should guide the choice of tasks for group work is that they require students to engage in cognitive activities more complex than rote learning or carrying out sequences of instructions. We see the prime function of group discussion to be collaboration in the development of rational thinking. In identifying the essential activity that enables small group talk to contribute to learning, Yager et al., (1985) use the phrase *cognitive rehearsal,* and include in this *intermittent summarizing* or *recalling* and the effect on the student's understanding of explaining to others. Peer support and tutoring may indeed contribute to rote learning or to familiarity with routine procedures (as appears to have been the case in some of the published research studies). In our view, however, the greatest value of group talk in any part of the curriculum lies in its contribution to understanding—though it is easy to lose sight of this when students are working in groups for some other reason, perhaps in order to share expensive equipment.

Group talk is most likely to contribute to learning when the students are engaged in *(a)* solving a problem, *(b)* interpreting texts, *(c)* making choices on the basis of evidence, *(d)* applying a principle to new cases (as in the *Spaceman* task), (e) planning and carrying out a productive activity to fulfill criteria which may either have been given or defined by the students themselves, or *(f)* exploring an issue for which there is no single correct answer. To take an example of *making choices on the basis of evidence,* several studies (Barnes 1976; Bennett and Cass 1988) have focused upon groups discussing the Saxon invasions of England in the fifth century. The students, having been taught about the Saxon way of life on the mainland of Europe, were presented with a large-scale map of part of the east coast of England and given the task of deciding where an invading party of Saxons would have set up their dwellings and what would have been their initial concerns in doing so. As in the other kinds of tasks listed above, this requires the analysis, rearrangement, and application of ideas and knowledge either already available to the students or presented to them by the teacher. Alternative suggestions need to be supported with arguments.

Most of the tasks in our study could be completed by means of discussion only. A task that includes the manipulation of objects or apparatus at once opens up for students an opportunity to discuss unexpected aspects of the world about them, though it also faces them with problems of managing not only the physical objects but their own social relationships when doing so. Students find it difficult to manipulate delicate apparatus and still think and talk about the meaning of the phenomena they are observing. During our research, one science teacher suggested a practical task that included the manipulation of an egg. Although a scientific issue was implicitly involved, this did not lead to useful discussion, since the students found it difficult to manage relationships in a way that would free one member of the group to carry out the delicate operation. It was this that dominated their discussion, not the issue that the teacher had in mind. Group work in science lessons frequently fails to support learning talk, because the manipulatory and social demands of the tasks outweigh the cognitive ones that are the overt purpose of the activity. There seems every reason in science to make a clear separation between occasions when groups are engaged in practical tasks and when they are engaged in discussing the meaning of what they have done or observed (Sutton 1992).

The nature and value of a discussion will be influenced both by the content of the task and by the tightness or looseness with which the directions are framed. When the teacher has a clear conception of the sequence of thought the group is to follow, he may wish to guide the discussions in this direction by means of a sequence of questions. On other occasions, even though the teacher may have a clear conception of an appropriate strategy and relevant evidence, there may be good reason not to predetermine the route to be followed. This difference in framing tasks can be illustrated from our materials. Of the tasks we used in the research, two, *Spaceman* and *The Pearl*, were contrasted in the tightness with which the task was defined.

The *Spaceman* task began with this preamble:

> We placed the corked bottle under a bell jar. We pumped the air out of the bell jar with a vacuum pump. Then the cork came out.

The discussion was structured first by two questions which required the students to recapitulate the principle arrived at during the preceding lesson.

1. Discuss among yourselves the relationship between the pressure in the BOTTLE with the pressure under the BELL JAR when all the air had been sucked out.

2. Why did the cork come out?

It should have been clear to all students from the first of these that they were expected to provide an explanation based upon the difference between the pressure in the bottle and the pressure in the bell jar: this part of the task was framed so as to provide tight constraints for their answers. The other two questions were:

3. If a piece of rock hit a spaceship and made a hole in it, what would happen to the air inside?

4. What would happen to the spaceman if he stepped out into space without a space suit on?

These are somewhat less tight, since though they define particular situations for the students to explain, they do not make it clear that differential pressure is again to be used as the basis for the explanation.

Compare this with the task based on Steinbeck's story *The Pearl*:

> In the introduction to The Pearl, John Steinbeck says that the story may be a parable, and that "perhaps everyone takes his own meaning from it."
>
> Discuss among yourselves what you have found in the story so far—the "good and bad things, and black and white things, and good and evil things," as Steinbeck says; and any points about the characters, the setting, and the way the book is written that you feel worth discussing.

In spite of the length of these instructions they do not rigidly constrain the replies. Moral issues from the story are to be discussed, but characters, setting, and style are also relevant. Moreover, "everyone takes his own meaning from it" is an invitation to the students to regard their own sense of relevance as paramount. However, it would have been possible to say no more than: "Talk about *The Pearl*." The question given provided the students with a framework that suggested lines of thought without imposing them.

If a teacher wishes students to engage in exploratory talk, it is important to indicate this in the phrasing of the task, by inviting a range of suggestions for the students themselves to evaluate. This emphasizes the process of discussion rather than particular conclusions to be reached. Since schools tend to emphasize *right answers*, students need encouragement to feel their way through difficult ideas and to explore half-formed intuitions. The reader will remember from page 50 the group who reached in their discussion of *The Pearl* an expression of shared enjoyment ("Shuper!") that no teacher could have planned for. This group's success reflects, of course, not merely the framing of the task but the value their English teacher had placed upon exploratory talk in previous lessons. The kind of explicitness often demanded of children in their written work, polished and revised for presentation, implicitly devalues the exploration of half-understood ideas, yet it is these latter which represent growth-points for future understanding.

It is not our intention to imply a preference for tasks which have no more than a loose structure; in our view the kind of task chosen should be matched to the particular kind of learning required at that moment. There is no universal principle to be enunciated which would guide a teacher in deciding whether a task should be defined tightly or loosely, for this should be influenced by the nature of the material to be learned, the level of the students' understanding, and the amount of time available. When a teacher sets up group work in order to place more emphasis on the journey of learning than on some prespecified destination, it is done to develop his students' ability to think and their confidence in attempting to make sense of complex issues. The task questions can therefore be framed so that students provide not one but several proposals or explanations and go on to produce arguments that can be advanced in support of each. Moreover, when a teacher asks questions, whether of the groups or on other occasions, this will powerfully inform the students whether he is more interested in right answers or the strategies by which valid answers may be arrived at.

On other occasions, teachers may reasonably wish to ensure that discussion does indeed focus on a concept or principle they wish to teach, and this may persuade them to provide guidance in the form of questions. Committees of adults find an agenda a useful aid in guiding the progress of a discussion, though they are often able to insist they control its contents. It can be argued that a tight series of questions performs this same function for a group of learners. Curricular subjects differ in the sharpness with which the knowledge to be learned has been predetermined; modern language or science teachers are more likely to have a sharply defined agenda than teachers of English literature or of social studies, subjects that leave both teacher and students more freedom to utilize knowledge from outside school (Bernstein 1971). In our research, it seemed that teachers chose to set loose tasks when their students had available much everyday knowledge that was relevant— as in *The Pearl* and *Gang Violence*—but tended to set tighter topics in science, when the explanations they wanted were more removed from everyday ways of looking at things. Other concerns too are likely to influence the tightness with which tasks are defined. For example, if particular students have been uncooperative, their behavior can influence the choice, since a tight sequence of tasks to be completed in a visible form will act as a means of control.

One danger inherent in breaking down the task into small steps is that since the teacher is carrying out the essential analysis, he is doing the thinking for the students. In such a case the principles which guided the teacher's sequence of questions would not be available to the students, which means that they would not have to penetrate far into the topic. Indeed Slavin (1990, 95) includes "cooperative planning by students" as one of the four essential elements in the approach called *group investigation*. (This was also a required part of the work in Design and Technology outlined in the previous section.) It is all to easy for the teacher who tries to guide discussion by tightly framing the questions to make inappropriate assumptions about the students' knowledge and insight and about their ability to apply these to the matter in hand. The teacher may have in mind a clear logical progression from given information to required conclusions, but the learners may need to go by a more circuitous route, using information and experience that would seem peripheral to the teacher. The best series of questions is one that helps the students structure their discussion without predetermining its route.

If students are given as much opportunity to control their own learning as they are able and willing to accept, this enables them to match their learning activities with their current needs. If a teacher knows that members of a class already have a good grasp of a topic, it will encourage her or him to leave the students more freedom to control the content of their discussion.

Teachers will take all these considerations into account when framing tasks: fortunately compromise between very tight and very loosely framed tasks is possible. From time to time opportunities should be provided for discussion in which participants discover what to talk about in the course of doing so. This gives them valuable experience and signals to them that not all knowledge is so esoteric that students cannot penetrate it for themselves.

Our research led us to another principle we can recommend to teachers: however tightly you decide to frame the task it is always worthwhile to append an open invitation to discuss other related matters. This can take the form of: "Finally, are there any other matters connected with this that seem to you to be worth discussing?" Even the most experienced teacher cannot predict all the problems of understanding that face a group of students in understanding new material. Teachers have the responsibility of making available to students the traditional ways of thinking in that school subject but should not forget the private and idiosyncratic problems they may have to deal with on the way. We found that students often see relevant possibilities when given apparatus to manipulate. Though this is often no more than strengthening their intuitive grasp of physical principles, some students are able to use apparatus for trying out hypotheses of their own. Like the group discussing *Spaceman*, from whose discussion we quoted on page 60 in Chapter 3, they see possibilities that the teacher has not foreseen, and talk about important issues related to those specified in the task. Such independent learning deserves to be encouraged.

There is much to be said for making all instructions available to students in written form since it enables them to refresh their memories easily—and also satisfies the needs of those who were not listening when the teacher was speaking. For the research we provided cards or slips of paper, but the busy teacher may find it easier to pin or write up a shorter task on a blackboard. (There will be many occasions when group talk is devoted to investigating documentary evidence or works of literature, and in that case the need for every student to have a copy can hardly be in doubt.)

The Composition of Groups

There has been a good deal of discussion during the last two decades of the most effective way of grouping students for collaborative talk. Some teachers allow the students to choose whom they work with, in the belief that friends will be more supportive of one another and that this will avoid clashes of personality within the groups. However, learning in small group talk derives primarily from the speaker's need to make his or her meaning explicit. This requires some differences of perspective within the group and with it the willingness to question and even to challenge the views of other members. Groups of friends sometimes pursue consensus at the expense of a rigorous examination of the topic in hand, for the maintenance of their friendship can become their primary goal. For example, when Group 12 at William Byrd School was accounting for the cork's flying out of the bottle (in the *Spaceman* task) members said:

15. **Teresa:** So that um made it possible for the cork to come out then.

16. **Nicola:** Well it didn't actually come out it were forced out really.

17. **Teresa:** Yeah.

18. **Nicola:** And there were all pressure, all the way round it, all them little particles floating about.

19. **Teresa:** Yeah.

20. **Nicola:** They were forcing the cork to come out anyway.

21. **Teresa:** Mm.

In this exchange Teresa was primarily providing social support, encouraging Nicola to continue, when she would have been better responding critically to what her friend was saying. When the desire for consensus leads to such vagueness, friendship grouping is not to be recommended. Bennett and Cass (1988) found that groups mixed in ability engaged in more interactions than those that were homogeneous and that their members were more able later to support their group's findings with appropriate reasons. It seems that the requirement to explain benefits both the explainer and the questioner and that questions are asked more readily when the children themselves recognize some members of the group as unofficial experts. Nevertheless, there is no reason to fear that able students will lose from taking part in group work: in their study, Bennett and Cass (1988) found that students described as *high attainers* achieved most whichever group they were in.

One issue that must concern all teachers is the danger that some students in the groups may be marginalized (Cohen et al. 1990). There is evidence to show that some students are effectively excluded from group talk, since whenever they make statements or ask questions they are ignored. (Webb 1982, in a study of group work in junior high school mathematics, found only one significant correlation—that between asking questions without receiving answers and low scores on tests.) This exclusion from the discussion may arise because the student is perceived by peers to be of very low ability: the evaluation procedures, formal and informal, that play such a central part in school activities inevitably mark some students as repeatedly unsuccessful, which influences not only their view of themselves but also the way they are treated by their peers. Members of some ethnic groups may be marginalized because of the overt or tacit racism of other students. Others may be unpopular for reasons that are not obvious, though teachers should always be on the lookout for signs that some students are being excluded. It is of course important that every student find a voice and receive an attentive hearing, but not only for him or her. Part of the effectiveness of group discussion arises from the need to interrelate and reconcile different perspectives, so it is important for all members of a group that a wide range of opinions is expressed and none excluded through an oppressive consensus. All students in a group should take the responsibility of seeing to it that all the others take a full part and gain as much from the discussion as they do. The advocates of *cooperative learning* make specific proposals for ensuring this, which are discussed in a later section.

For many boys and girls in their early teens, it seems that single sex groups are slightly more comfortable and less challenging than mixed ones. If students of this age are free to choose, most groups are likely to be single-sex, for at this age students seem to define as *friends* only members of their own sex. When a teacher insists on groups mixed in this sense, an important part of the task facing the group is working in an unfamiliar situation, but this is not to imply that such mixing should never take place. It is sometimes feared that girls will be marginalized by boys in the groups, but this does not always seem to happen. Bennett and Cass (1988) reported that the eleven- and twelve-year-old girls in their study talked more than the boys, even in those groups where they were outnumbered.

However, the task given to students in their research was in the field of history; we wonder whether the same would have been the case in some technical or scientific tasks. Bennett and Dunne (1992) found on the contrary that girls did speak less in groups where boys predominated; research into the effects of gender on participation unfortunately does not provide clear guidelines for teachers. Both the students' familiarity with working in small groups and their grasp of the material should influence any teacher who wonders whether to face the students with the additional social dilemmas consequent upon "mixed" grouping.

A different mixing of students was central to the monumental study reported by Sharan et al. (1984), which was as much intended to show that group work could help students of different ethnic groups to learn to respect one another through working together as to demonstrate that this is an effective way of learning for all students. "The Group Investigation methods strives to cultivate democratic participation and equitable distribution of speaking privileges to group members . . . " (p. 5). Other studies show that the need to explain to peers who are not intimates constitutes a challenge to speak explicitly which itself aids learning. These principles must therefore be balanced against the social gains that induce some teachers to allow students to work in friendship groups.

It will be clear from the foregoing paragraphs that there are strong reasons for ensuring that from time to time students work in groups that have been deliberately planned to mix them with classmates they would not necessarily have chosen to work with. Like adults, young people talk most openly with people they know well and trust, the talk being primarily oriented to sharing experiences and ideas, whereas with people they do not know so well they are likely to present a more public face (Watson and Potter 1962). But sharing, though valuable, may not provide the impetus to push their understanding to its limits; to encourage explicitness within exploratory talk, students need the challenge of communicating with others who do not precisely share their preconceptions and views. Friends may accept vague formulations which would be challenged by others, and we believe that this need to make explicit and redefine plays central part in learning, for the speaker even more than for the hearers.

It is our view that groups should seldom contain more than four students, for even a membership of five may lead to competition to speak, which makes it more likely that less confident members will take less part in the talks and some students be marginalized altogether. The fifth or sixth member of the group imposes strains upon the social organization which diverts the students from their main task. Some research suggests that three is the ideal number. For our first set of recordings we used groups of four, which worked admirably in most cases, but we noticed in one or two groups that when communication became difficult they tended to split into two pairs who talked separately. This was one reason why on our second set of recordings we worked with single-sex groups of three.

Alternative Models for Group Work

It is our view that teachers should be able to choose among a range of ways of setting up groups and framing tasks for them. However, a number of writers have prescribed quite precise models for managing group activities: these models, perhaps originally put forward for the purpose of controlling research, are in danger of fossilizing as *techniques*, and this raises matters of principle. In this section we discuss three of them—jigsaw, STAD, and group investigation—and contrast them with an eclectic approach designed by a teacher. Our own preference is for handing students as much responsibility as possible for guiding their learning, and whenever possible choosing material for discussion with the interest and challenge to provide an intrinsic incentive for them to complete the task as well as they can. However, we judge that our readers will wish to consider other forms of group organization besides those we advocate.

The jigsaw approach was developed by Aronson et al. (1978) in order to ensure that all participants in a group are equally involved in researching a given topic and equally have the opportunity to present the results to others in the role of expert. We now describe, however, a version of the jigsaw approach that has been used in England. The teacher, perhaps in consultation with students, chooses a topic, and within it a set of sub-topics that the students can be expected to investigate. For example, in a high school literature class, within the study of a novel there might be a range of sub-topics which include discussion of the significance of certain key episodes, the attitudes and motives of one or two characters, the importance of settings to the overall effect of the novel, and the author's probable intentions and values. Alternatively, in a history class different aspects of a historical event might be similarly identified, to be investigated from documentary evidence supplied by the teacher. Similarly, linked tasks can be devised in other subjects. The students begin in home groups and the sub-tasks are assigned so that in each home group there are several pairs of students who share the same sub-topic. The students first work in these pairs and then, when the teacher judges that enough preliminary work has been done, every pair joins another pair that has been working on the same topic. In these *topic* groups each pair presents the material and ideas that they have so far assembled, and the discussion then leads to a conflation of the two perspectives. In the version that most interests us, the students finally meet in a third set of groups in which each participant has a different concern. In this third group each of the students in turn reports the conclusions that he or she has reached in conjunction with others, thus giving everyone the opportunity to speak from the vantage point of being a quasi specialist. Finally each group is expected to reorganize and conflate its version of the material for presentation in some form to an audience, perhaps from outside the class.

STAD (Student Teams and Academic Divisions) refers to a form of cooperative learning that has been advocated by Slavin and his associates. It is focused more upon the mastery of information than upon inquiry or problem solving. The activity follows this sequence (Slavin 1990, 5):

1. The teacher presents new material to the class.

2. The groups of students, guided by worksheets, begin to learn the material, testing and instructing one another by rehearsal and other means until they are satisfied that all know the material well.

3. The students then answer individual quizzes without being allowed to help one another.

4. The quizzes are scored not competitively but as an improvement score for each student from a baseline established at the beginning of the unit or semester.

5. The improvement scores for each group are put together and all members of those groups which have shown overall improvement gain certificates and other rewards.

The purpose of the individual testing and the group scores is to ensure that all students take responsibility both for their own success in learning and for that of all other members of the group. This is intended to avoid the marginalizing of any student and to make certain that less able members of the group receive help from others. In contrast with the approach to collaborative learning that we recommend, the rewards offered are extrinsic, not derived from the intrinsic interest or challenge of the material to be learned. It is significant that a set of quiz items (in multiple choice format) provided as examples by Slavin (77) is made up of: the addition of simple fractions, the selection of a word (*good* or *well*) to fill a gap in a sentence, the symbol for a chemical compound, and the name of the capital of Canada. It is clear that STAD is designed for very different kinds of learning from those we investigated in our research, since it is focused upon memorizing and the adoption of conventions.

Group investigation, which is particularly associated with Shlomo Sharan and his associates, follows this sequence:

1. Students, working in group of two to six, which are mixed for ability and ethnic origin, choose to investigate sub-topics within an area selected by the teacher.

2. Each group, in consultation with the teacher, plans goals, tasks, and learning procedures appropriate to the sub-topic.

3. The plan is carried out, utilizing a variety of activities and skills which lead students to sources inside and outside the school. The teacher follows their work and offers assistance when necessary.

4. The group plans how the material the members have collected can be presented to the rest of the class.

5. Some or all of the groups present their material.

6. Each group's contribution to the overall task is evaluated by students and teacher in collaboration. Individual assessment can be included in this.

(Sharan et al. also allocated specific roles to group members; this practice we consider below.)

In a study of seventh grade students in Israel (Sharan et al. 1984), group investigation was shown on the basis of test results to lead to better learning than STAD, which in turn was more effective than class teaching in several parts of the curriculum. Slavin (1992) holds a similar opinion:

> Traditional group work, in which students are encouraged to work together but are given little structure and few incentives to do so, has been repeatedly found to have small or non-existent effects on students' learning. (30)

It might be thought that this and other research studies that have proclaimed the superiority of tightly structured group work would persuade us to reject the methods used by the teachers in our study. There are two reasons why this is not the case. First, we are not convinced that the methods of testing learning outcomes used in these studies provide a valid reflection of the kinds of learning we are interested in; for example, Sharan et al. tested achievement by multiple-choice single-word questions, even when the achievement in question was *high level* understanding of literature. Second, the focus of interest has been on what the teachers did in setting up the work, while the content and nature of the group talk has seldom been investigated. Without more detailed information about this interaction it is difficult to be certain which learning activities are being preferred and which rejected. It is our view that teachers need not only to know how to set up group work but also how to diagnose its state of health, so as to guide their decisions about when and how to intervene.

Many researchers whose work we have referred to advise teachers to assign roles to members of each group. Yager et al. (1985) recommend that the role of *leader* be rotated regularly about the group, each leader having the responsibility of summarizing the content of the lesson while the other members of the group give help by probing, reminding, discussing, and improving the account. Partly to obviate the danger that some students will be marginalized, Cohen et al. (1990) proposed that each member of a group have an assigned role, as facilitator, checker, reporter, supervisor, and so on, and suggested games by which students could be trained in the roles. We believe that all students need to learn how to take responsibility for the social and cognitive demands of group work but do not believe that devising artificial roles will forward the development of shared responsibility.

We conclude this section by describing a fourth method which derives not from an academic research team but from a schoolteacher. Drawing on ideas from other teachers and from her reading, Tonya Dix decided to put into effect an inquiry model of learning with her third grade students in order to improve their reading strategies (Dix 1993).

> In my classroom students self-select into discussion groups according to book titles . . . The students meet to decide what the reading assignment will be and when they will meet to have their discussions. After they have made these decisions, students read the agreed upon pages individually or with a partner. While reading, students record their responses to the literature in their journals, including things they want to discuss with the group, reactions to the story, predictions of what will come next, and so on. When the groups meet to share and discuss their responses, they . . . may choose to talk about character development or plot interpretation, offer their opinions with reasons to support them, or clarify a point. Very often, students make connections between the literature they are discussing and other books . . . and their own or others' life experience. (316)

The teacher's contribution is crucial: both in introducing this note-making and in the course of other work on literature such as class discussions, she had established in her students a set of expectations about how to talk about literature. These expectations shaped what was noted down for discussion, and therefore the focus of the group talk. The success of this work made it clear that in some areas of the curriculum very young students can take over responsibility for deciding their needs as learners, so long as their teacher helps them to find an appropriate framework in which to do so.

Roles and Responsibilities for the Teacher

In discussing collaborative inquiry we said that it requires of a teacher the willingness at times to step outside the role of academic authority and to take part in finding out. Teaching in this way requires great flexibility from teachers, since they must match their role to the requirements of the occasion. Slavin (1990) sums up these roles as *resource* and *facilitator*, yet there may be occasions when a teacher needs to take on other roles, such as discussant, instructor in a technique that the students find they need for the task in hand, or chairperson of class discussion. Such fluidity of role can seem threatening to any teachers who have become used to identifying their professional competence with close control over the public events of the classroom. Group discussion does not necessarily go the way that a teacher would choose to lead it. Students may pursue lines of thought that seem irrelevant, or that twist and turn upon themselves in a way quite unlike the orderly progress of a teacher's lesson notes. When a teacher adopts group work he implicitly relaxes tight control over public events, and this can threaten the sense of competence even of an experienced teacher. He is thus exchanging control of public events—of public communication–for the students' closer involvement in the subject matter, an involvement that cannot be taken for granted behind the public appearance of participation. It is only the public events that can be controlled when a teacher faces a class, and not the focus or quality of the students' attention.

We have no doubt of the importance in the success of small group work of the students' wider experience of school, their previous experience of exploratory talk, the way they interpret the purpose of the work, the attitudes of other teachers, and the tacit messages sent by the school about how far students are valued and trusted. Much of this may be beyond the influence of one teacher, but he can see to it that students understand the view of learning that is implicit in talking to learn, and that they have opportunities to reflect not only on their progress as learners but also upon their roles and responsibilities in the running of the groups. It sometimes happens too that particular students show no comprehension of what discussion involves and either allocate decisions to group members to make individually or adopt a television interview format which leads to statement without any interaction or exchange of views. To achieve collaborative inquiry it is necessary to do everything possible to counterbalance the long-term effects of the individualism and competition that play so large a part in schooling.

It is essential to prepare and support students for participation in groups; every writer on the subject emphasized that. In the previous section we illustrated how a third grade teacher saw to it that her students were talking about a novel in a manner that would advance their understanding and empathy. It is important also to help them develop the necessary social skills. Slavin quotes from Smith, Johnson, and Johnson (1981) a set of *rules* to guide students' participation:

1. I am critical of ideas not people.
2. I remember that we are all in this together.
3. I encourage everyone to participate.
4. I listen to everyone's ideas, even if I do not agree with them.
5. I restate what someone said if it is not clear.
6. I try to understand both sides of the issue.
7. I first bring out all the ideas, then I put them together.

Although this list seems to be focused on a particular view of discussion (Do *all* topics have "both sides"? Would not some ideas eventually be rejected?) and would not necessarily be presented to all of the students in this form, it provides a useful beginning for discussion. There is much to be said for asking groups to reflect upon their experience of working together in order to determine what helped and what hindered progress and to use this discussion to formulate a similar set of principles for collaboration. It will be necessary to return to this from time to time to keep these principles before students, so that they accept the responsibility, for example, of ensuring that no member of the group is pushed to the margins of the discussion and that personal animosity does not damage the work of the group.

When students are to have the opportunity to choose their own tasks, it is essential to give them support in doing so by helping them consider a range of alternatives. The purpose is of course to make sure the task they set themselves is one they can learn from.

One problem that can beset students in early adolescence is that their first choices may be dominated by imagery from the worlds of popular music, sport, and fashion, reinforced by peer group norms that they find difficult to escape. If students choose such topics they may be locked into conventions of subject matter and discourse style—derived from the popular music press, for example—that discourage analysis and critical thinking. On the other hand, older students can with appropriate preparation and support be enabled to look critically at some aspects of the culture they participate in, perhaps by analyzing the contents and perspectives of a group of magazines, for example. At the beginning of a larger-scale study in groups the students need to be introduced to new ways of looking at a topic which will generate other possible lines of thought and a mode of discourse for approaching them. The presentation of material on film or in documentary form, demonstrations in a science laboratory, talks by adults from outside school about dilemmas that occur in their work, or a visit to an institution—perhaps a factory or an old people's home—any of these can be used to display a range of new possibilities for investigation and discussion. Time should be spent on preliminary discussion of the students' ideas for a project, and then on a first rough sketch of how the topics might be pursued. The teacher's presence and advice is critical at this stage, since it is now possible tactfully to direct groups away from choices that are likely to prove unrewarding or too difficult to complete. Some teachers use a *topic board* on the wall of their classroom, on which each group progressively records its developing conception of the nature of its task and how group members are pursuing it and also a tracking sheet on which they record their day-to-day activities (Wells et al. 1990, 115).

As we show in Chapter 3, one way students can improve their views of a topic is by taking alternative viewpoints into account, building from the interplay of diversity a way of understanding that subsumes both. The most successful groups, far from rejecting divergent viewpoints, made use of one another's opinions, though with modifications. But some students found it difficult to assign any validity to views expressed by persons with whom they disagreed. From time to time groups meet problems in their relationship with one another, and it is important that action be taken when this is happening. In one group personal animus played a part:

12. **Lesley:** Well, because they're bored.

13. **Glenys:** You always have to get your point through, don't you?

Later Glenys retaliated:

19. Lesley: They, y'know, want to show off.

20. Glenys: You've said that six times now.

This antagonism broke out on several other occasions during the time we recorded this group and certainly impeded the progress of the discussion. The aggression expressed by another group seemed to be generated more by the task's demands than by existing rivalries. All four members of the group wanted to take on the practical task of chipping a hole in the shell of an egg, and those who did not do so expressed their frustration by criticizing and offering unwanted advice to the boy who had taken it on. This led to pushing and abuse. It may well be necessary for a teacher to deal with such tensions in public, asking the class to discuss repair strategies, since it is better for resentment and jealousy to be expressed under the teacher's control than for it to mar the work of a group. It was perhaps significant that both of these groups were at Wickhouse School where group work seemed to be unfamiliar and where the teachers had not, so far as we knew, explained to students why they were being asked to work in this way.

One of the most difficult demands upon teachers is to relax their normal control of the students' attention and trust them to focus upon the given task. Observation of the groups is essential, usually in as unobtrusive a way as possible. At times, however, it is useful to sit near a group, avoiding eye contact, so that the students know you are listening but do not wish to be brought into the conversation. It is best not to take part unless the group's work is being impeded by a problem they cannot deal with. The teacher's presence can support and refocus the students' talk; the teacher's participation radically changes its nature and not necessarily for the better. It usually ceases to be an exchange and becomes directed toward the teacher's approval, the language taking on the abbreviated patterns usual when students assume that it is not necessary to expound their thinking for the teacher (Barnes 1976). From time to time it is well to record a group for replay at another time. Although this is time-consuming, it enables the teacher to consider at leisure the success of the tasks and any intervention or changes needed. (This is discussed in more detail in Chapter 5.) Moreover, it is useful to play back carefully selected passages for discussion either by the group in question, or (with their permission) by the class as a whole, since this can lead to focused attention on the conditions for successful talk. However, some teachers believe that, for fear of damaging students' self-respect, one should only play back students' talk in situations where they can be anonymous.

In this chapter we have necessarily focused attention upon technical considerations in setting up and managing group work, but we must reaffirm that what we have described is not a mere technique. There is no *best method* for group work: the subject matter, the task, the grouping, the materials used, the placing within a larger sequence or unit—all should be decided in the light of an educational purpose relevant to those students at that particular time. Group talk can only be justified insofar as it leads to more effective learning, and moreover to learning of a different kind, which strengthens the students' capacity for thinking constructively and critically both for their own purposes and as members of a group. We live at a time when such critical collaboration is greatly needed in the world in which students are already youthful participants.

Chapter Five

Studying Group Talk

We have made it plain that beginning to set up opportunities for students to learn through collaborative talk is much more than a change in classroom technique, since it requires of teachers a qualitative change in their perception of their own roles and those of students in the processes of teaching and learning. Thus for most teachers to change the grouping of students in their classes is only the first step; they need not only to experience the consequent events but to reinterpret them through the kinds of reflection that can lead to delicate changes in their own participation in lessons and possibly in their attitudes to students and their learning. For this reason it has been argued by various theorists, especially Stenhouse (1975), that all teachers should be researchers. That is, they should habitually consider their own teaching and its effects in a detached but critical light, if possible collecting evidence that would support this.

This is why in this chapter we suggest ways for teachers to study the conditions, processes, and results of enabling students to engage in collaborative inquiry. We envisage three ways in which such study can take place: the informal monitoring by a teacher of her own teaching; collaborative study by a group of teachers as a contribution to their professional development, and steps in research for a higher degree. The three overlap in some ways, but there are also differences associated with their different purposes. In this chapter we will discuss them separately.

Informal Monitoring

> Only those who reflect on their experiences develop competence—
> ability to deal with new situations similar to those they have al-
> ready experienced. An unreflecting, purely habitual action does
> not transcend what has once been learned. (Florin, Göranzon, and
> Sällström 1991, 23)

Reflection on practice is a powerful means for improving that practice (Schön, 1983). The practical means to aid reflection need not be
complicated. Rather, its power lies in the nature of the questions a
practitioner asks about her practice; and in the extent to which the
resulting answers are based on a clear-sighted analysis of what she
actually does, day by day, in the classroom.

Informal monitoring helps teachers pose reflective questions
about their everyday use of small group discussions and in doing so
enhance their ability to design collaborative learning that will extend their students. One of the least formal modes of such reflection
is to work alone, or perhaps with an interested colleague, looking at
what happens in the groups. There are several questions a teacher
working in this way might want to ask. At the outset a teacher may
want simply to check whether a particular task designed for group
discussion *worked*, whether students are coping with the demands
of small group work and whether the groupings used are causing
difficulties. To do this it may be sufficient to review the group task
with the students and to listen to the recorded discussion of one or
more of the groups in the class, making notes on impressions and
pointers for the future. Even monitoring at this level of informality
is likely to yield some unexpected insights. Teachers hear less of
their students than their students hear of them, so listening to a tape
of group discussion provides a valuable opportunity to get to know
one's students better. Besides providing evidence about the group
talk itself, listening to tapes of group discussions aids diagnosis of
the range of levels of understanding in the class of an issue that has
been taught and also helps diagnose the state of learning of particular individuals. These insights, which can be used to redesign future teaching, identify the need for remedial work and so on, can be
grouped into the following areas:

1. By listening to recordings a teacher can check whether students
   have fully comprehended material presented to them in class
   and whether they have grasped essential principles and can
   apply them. Recording the students has the obvious advantage
   that it constitutes a permanent record of what the students said,
   so the teacher may stop it, play it back, check and re-check what

she is hearing. The moment-by-moment demands of teaching leave no time to consider carefully what the students are saying so that impressions gained in class about the nature of the students' understanding are only too liable to be forgotten.

2. It may at times be more important, however, to understand how one's pupils are thinking than what they are thinking. The route by which students reach their conclusions is often very different from that taken by the teacher. They make links with unexpected areas of knowledge, as when Group 15 tried to explain flat fish in terms of pressure, thus showing that they saw pressure as exerted downwards only. They may use unexpected strategies: in setting the *Steve's Letter* task we expected a discussion of appropriate styles, but the students chose to fill in hypothetical situations ("He might be an old man, a friend like. . . .") as if the context we had given was too thin to make a judgment possible. Thus there is value in understanding how students arrive at their conclusions which is quite separate from deciding whether the conclusions themselves are acceptable.

3. Information can also be gained about the suitability of tasks and materials for the students. The concepts may be too difficult or too obvious; the pupils may need new information or more experience with other examples; the questions may be ambiguous, or need to be directed more tightly or more loosely. In general, listening to students who are using a work-sheet suggests how it might be revised before it is used again.

4. The teacher can monitor the social characteristics of her successful discussion groups, so as to improve future ones. We have discussed single-sex versus mixed groups, and the influence upon the group's talk of members' familiarity with each other, but we have not been able to give any conclusive recommendations that would hold for all students. Listening in on the groups helps the teacher to work out the most appropriate and helpful way of setting up groups from her particular class.

5. Another spin-off from listening to pupils' discussions is that they often show skills in the discussion groups that go unnoticed, or are not called for, in the full class. In our experience, teachers have gained new insights into their pupils' strengths as well as their weaknesses by listening to group talk.

6. The final reason we can suggest for a teacher to monitor pupils' discussion groups is to gain insights on the effect of her own participation in those groups. A common way of using small group work within the lesson framework is for the teacher to

present material to the full class, then to ask the class to perform some operations on this material while working in small groups, and then for the teacher to move around the class from group to group, questioning, encouraging, explaining. But what does her intervention do? She may feel the need to modify the way she participates in these groups when she has the opportunity to listen to and reconsider her teaching strategies.

So far we have been thinking largely of a teacher working individually to enhance her understanding of the way small groups work and to make future discussions in her classroom more effective. However, if groups of students can enhance their understanding by working together, so can teachers. The UK's National Oracy Project, which worked by setting up groups within and between schools to investigate various aspects of the place of spoken language in school curricula, was shaped by a similar view of how best to advance the professional competence of teachers. The National Oracy Project's local groups were concerned with a far wider range of topics than collaborative talk in small groups, but group talk had a high profile in the interests of many participating teachers, so that it is possible to extract from the project's publications, local and national, many examples of informal investigations of small group talk by individuals or groups which can serve as examples of topics that teachers have studied.

Groups of teachers investigated students' understanding when they worked together on tasks involving mathematical apparatus, and there was much interest in the talk of students around a computer, since the frequently very cryptic exchanges had generated anxiety about its effectiveness for learning. Some schools were interested in identifying contexts and tasks that would encourage bilingual students to take more part in group talk, including enabling them to use their mother tongue when it was not the dominant language of the classroom. Story telling as a focus of teachers' attentions appears many times in the project's publications; younger students often found it easier to tell stories through puppets or toy animals. One group recorded young students' role play as travel agents and their clients, with the intention of identifying gains in confidence, in the ability to adopt an appropriate style, and in explicitness in making their meaning clear.

Teachers of various subjects—science, mathematics, history, geography, English—took part in the project. For example, a geography teacher involved groups of pupils in planning an imaginary leisure center for the area. A group of teachers in one school set out to identify the contexts and teaching styles that would support and encourage students to take on the responsibility of problem solving in groups. The contribution of talk to writing was a common interest, and sequences of drafts as well as recorded discussion were assembled. (The influence of writing upon talk was apparently not seen as problematic.) Gender roles proved to be a commonly chosen focus for teachers of older students; one teacher reported setting up group discussion of male and female stereotypes as a preparation for reading a novel, *The Turbulent Term of Tyke Tyler* by Gene Kemp, which is intended to challenge the reader's stereotyped expectations; this work went so well that she went on to have her students analyze literature for younger students, including school textbooks, from the point of view of stereotyping. Many teachers of English carried out informal studies of the way their students discussed poems.

While many teachers inclined toward the study of practical aspects of their teaching, groups led by project coordinators—teachers seconded to lead the local project's activities—were more inclined to consider theoretical issues. One group asked itself what would constitute evidence of progression and development in speaking and listening in group work and went on to make this the basis for an approach to the assessment now required by the UK government. Other groups identified a range of different functions of talk and set out to illustrate and discuss possible markers of development in each of them. Several investigated older students' attitudes to group inquiry, provoking discussion by giving students a set of statements about talk to put into an agreed order of validity. (A common concern of project members was how to change other teachers' attitudes to students' talk; one cited an occasion when a colleague said to a student, "Don't talk. Mr.[a visitor] has come to see your best work.") Three of these working parties wrote papers that eventually appeared in a project publication (Norman 1992). One group began by discussing examples of teachers and students asking questions and were persuaded by these particular examples to move on to a general discussion of the role of questioning in lessons (Brierley et al. 1992). Basing their analysis on five cases, Des-Fountain and Howe (1992) identified systematically the conditions that enable students to "work on understanding" in groups. One group began by considering the dictum that teachers should "present to the child a variety of appropriate audiences," but went far beyond that framework by identifying eight modes of contribution open to a teacher who decides to enter an ongoing group discussion (Corden 1992).

Whether one is working alone or sharing examples with other interested colleagues will make a difference in decisions about such issues as whether it is necessary to transcribe recordings of the discussions. A teacher working alone may feel it is sufficient to listen to such recordings once or twice, maybe returning to give more attention to certain sections that seem especially interesting, for whatever reason. After listening, pondering and making notes if that seems helpful, the teacher may wipe the tape for reuse—although some teachers may wish to keep taped examples of group discussions for future reference, perhaps accumulating examples of group tasks and group discussions into an ongoing portfolio record of teaching. If she is working alone and will be listening to the tape soon after the recording was made, the quality of the recording is not too important—knowledge of the context and immediacy of memory will help make sense of it. But this memory soon fades so any teacher who views informal monitoring of group discussions as a long-term project will want to ensure recording quality and a level of documentation that will mean the recording is still intelligible at some point in the future. It can be helpful to listen to some extracts with the students and to keep a note of the points they raise. This is a way of enhancing the students' confidence in their ability to collaborate in groups. By listening to recordings with the students the teacher shows how important she considers this independent work to be. She can also point out to the students what it is she considers valuable about what they are doing.

Where teachers are working together in interest groups, it will be more important to make sure that the quality of the recording is good enough for outsiders to understand and to keep explanatory notes about the context. We wouldn't recommend that teachers attempt to make written transcriptions of discussions as a whole, nor is it necessary to make detailed and highly accurate transcriptions showing pauses, lengths of silences, and so on. Rather, we would suggest identifying, during one or two listenings, those sections of the dialogue that seem to be significant for the learning process. Two or three teachers listening together are likely to produce a varied set of comments on what the students were doing in their group talk and out of discussion among the group of teachers, a more complex understanding of the students' learning may be formed than if a teacher listens alone. Whether working individually or in a group, one of the features of informal monitoring is its flexibility. It can be initiated or stopped at will as the demands of social, personal and professional life vary. A teacher can sample group discussions as and when it seems interesting—but also when it seems possible. There is no purpose other than those the teacher decides for herself and no external timetable or outsiders' requirements to meet.

What might one look for when listening to recordings? Teachers' interests are likely to be rather different from those of researchers so that the category systems that have been developed for research purposes may conceal what teachers want to know instead of making it clear. However, it is sometimes difficult when faced with a new recording of group talk to decide where to begin to discuss it, so we offer the following questions as potential starting points:

1. What are the students doing in their talk? What are they *using talk for?* This is often a useful starting point since it can lead to discussion both of the content of what is said and of the social processes going on.

2. What signs are there of learning going on? This can be approached by analyzing either the characteristics of the speech—or by analyzing the sequence of thought. It also raises questions about what is meant by *learning*, and this can often be usefully discussed in relation to a particular conversation.

3. Talk is sometimes used for *presenting* ideas that are already well-formed, and at other times for *exploring* and shaping thought in new ways, that is, new to the speaker. Where do your discussions lie on the *presenting-exploring* dimension? How do you know?

4. Are the pupils working together in constructing lines of thought? The cognitive strategies we discussed in Chapter 3 could be used as a basis for looking at their thinking. How explicit do they make their viewpoints, especially when they differ from one another? Does this seem to matter?

5. What devices do the students use to organize their social relationships with one another? Which of the social skills illustrated in Chapter 2 do they display?

6. What seems to influence the relative success or failure of these discussions in promoting useful learning? What part in this is played by the subject matter and its relationship to what the students already know? What part is played by apparatus, computers, pictures, objects, maps, texts, etc.? Did the way in which the task was set prove helpful? Might the talk have been better if the students had been differently grouped?

Studying Talk as Part of Professional and School Development

Informal monitoring of the kind we have outlined here is likely to have a local and practical focus. Here are these individual students in this class working on particular small group tasks that their teacher has devised: how are they doing, what is going on, how could the teacher better support their learning next time? In our next section we turn to studying group talk for the purposes of professional development. This doesn't mean that we think informal monitoring such as we have just outlined doesn't aid a teacher's development as a practitioner, quite the contrary. However, looking at group talk in the context of participation in an in-service course or in a school-based curriculum development project marks a shift to a perspective which necessarily must encompass more general features in its sight than the local matter of teaching these particular students in this way on this occasion. It is to these wider purposes that we turn next.

There is no clear line to be drawn between listening to the talk of one's students in order to monitor their participation and progress, and doing so in collaboration with other teachers in order to develop a more general understanding of the role of talk in classroom learning. Collaboration with colleagues in the development of professional understanding greatly enhances the benefits to be gained and makes the activity itself more enjoyable. The present authors have themselves worked with groups of colleagues to study classroom talk and to monitor the implementation of curriculum development schemes. It is a challenging and exciting way to enhance understanding of what goes on in lessons and the role of communication in learning.

Groups of teachers may decide to work together in studying students' talk during learning in various institutional contexts. Colleagues may collaborate as part of their school's in-service program, or teachers from different schools may meet as members of a professional association, such as the Association for Science Education or the National Council for Teachers of English. They may be members of a curriculum development project: one of the present authors some years ago was director of a funded project (called *Children as Readers*) that persuaded groups of teachers in various parts of the United Kingdom to meet on their own time to investigate teaching and learning in English literature, some of them choosing to study small group talk about literature. More formally, tutors responsible for in-service courses often decide that their students should carry out studies of classroom language in collaboration before reporting them individually as part of the course requirements. Moreover a school, as part of the process of developing a new curriculum, can decide to set up working groups of colleagues whose work could include sampling classroom talk in small groups as evidence of the progress of the innovation. Some curriculum development initiatives are supported by staff development programs to support teachers in new ways of teaching. We can give two examples to which one of the authors has contributed. In the first, the teaching advisor in a UK local education authority brought together deputy heads and senior subject specialists from a number of schools within the authority's area to develop policies and practices on language across the curriculum in each of the participating schools. A number of residential professional development workshops were held over a period of about three years to support this school-based curriculum development process. Another local education authority in a different part of the United Kingdom supported small teams of teachers—two or three from each of a number of schools—to participate in a university-based in-service education program in which the teams of teachers conducted action research on linked facets of a curriculum development project chosen for its relevance to their school. Issues relating to small group teaching and the promotion of pupil talk in learning were pursued by one member of such a team and the outcomes were not only implemented in that school but also were disseminated to teams of teachers from other schools participating in the in-service curriculum development scheme.

Whether at the whole school or subject level, major curriculum development will probably be accompanied by an evaluation study, perhaps conducted informally within the school or perhaps involving external evaluators. At any of these levels of formality of professional and school development, it may be appropriate for groups of teachers to work together, perhaps with outsiders, to study students' talk in small groups. Most of what is recommended in this section refers to all such groups, whether they are led by a tutor or whether a group of teachers is working together as action researchers.

The first step for such a group is to settle either upon an initial focus to get the study under way, or (more ambitiously) to choose an overall topic to be investigated. For example, a group of teachers working within the *Children as Readers* project decided at their first meeting that they wanted to understand why it was that older adolescents sometimes declined to take an active part in discussions of literature led by the teacher, even when the topic was a novel they had enjoyed. Ignoring other possible explanations, the members of the group decided to find out how their students talked about books when alone in small groups to see whether it would throw light on this lack of participation. (It did!) This issue gave shape to the collection of recorded material and to a series of meetings that lasted for more than a year and culminated in a report written by three members of the group and published in a national journal for

English teachers. However, if a common interest cannot be found at the first meeting, it is possible to work from meeting to meeting, at the end of each choosing a focus for the next.

If an overall topic has been chosen by the group or by the tutor (or by both in consultation) it is possible for all members of a group to collect parallel material at the outset. Even if the same issue is being addressed by all members of the group, useful contrasts will be introduced if the recordings are made with students of different ages, or in different curricular areas, or in the course of different activities. When this work is being done as part of a short course—perhaps a residential week—it will be essential for all recordings to be done in advance, which means preplanning by the tutor to ensure that productive contrasts are built in to the material. On one occasion all the US teachers planning to attend a short vacation course at an English university were asked to bring recordings made in their own classrooms. The preliminary instructions for the course included:

> Take a group of not more than five students and set them a task that requires discussion. The task can be based on apparatus or written materials supplied to the group, and can—if you wish—relate to ongoing work you are doing with the class. Leave them on their own during the initial discussion for as long as they feel they need to complete the task.
>
> For the second stage you yourself should join the group, and should endeavour (a) to elicit from the students the substance of their discussion, and (b) to improve and extend their understanding by your own contributions and questions.

(The remainder of the instructions referred to the ages of students and to recording and transcription.) The purpose of making the recordings was to institute among members of the course informed reflection on the relationship of small group talk to other kinds of talk led by the teacher. The issue selected by the tutor (one of the present writers) was the difficulty experienced even by the most skillful teacher of tuning in to the individual learning needs of students. It usually turns out that comparing the two recordings shows a wide gap between the issues the students discuss and those the teacher had expected to be relevant. The teacher is not, of course, in some way *wrong*; she will have important curricular priorities but these may not match the immediate needs of some of the students. Both are important if the classroom discussions are to support learning effectively.

However, though such prerecording of similar material may be essential for short courses, there are strong arguments against it when teachers are meeting occasionally over a long period. (We are envisaging a group that meets perhaps every three or four weeks. This gives enough time for preparing new material but not enough to lose continuity of interest.) The discussion during the first one or two meetings generates new understanding of the issues involved that will shape and give focus to subsequent recordings, so that insights become cumulative. For this reason, it is better not to plan all the collection of material at the outset. We recommend that whenever possible every meeting should end by devoting time to planning the next. A useful pattern is for two or three members in turn to undertake to collect material that will take the discussion further, throwing light on issues raised but not so far sufficiently discussed. (We suggest that the responsibility should not be given to one person alone, since if she is unable for some reason to complete the recording and attend the next meeting, this may threaten the survival of the group, unless there is other material held in reserve.) The two or three *presenters* would take responsibility not only for producing recordings and partial transcripts, but also for leading discussion. By *leading discussion* we do not mean that they should present a paper but that they should give preliminary thought to the issues raised by their recordings which they can then present in question form to the group in order to provoke discussion. A pre-prepared paper would bring the danger of closing down the thinking of other members of the group, rather than bringing their diverse experience and values into the group's discussion. It is best, but not essential, that the *presenters* meet before the following meeting to discuss how they will organise their material.

Let us take an imaginary example. Several teachers have agreed on a series of meetings to discuss the teaching of a topic in science, perhaps *light*. They want to use small group discussion (1) to find what are their students' existing preconceptions about how we see, what reflection and refraction are, and how cameras work, and (2) to find out whether a series of practical tasks which one of them has devised for student groups will indeed improve understanding of these matters. At the first meeting they discuss their own experiences of teaching about light and decide that since their students' existing preconceptions seem at times to provide a barrier to understanding they will begin by discovering more about what these are. Three members offer to make recordings of their own students talking in groups and present them at the next meeting.

The three teachers agree to make their own recordings and then listen to them together before the next meeting of the whole group. Separately each teacher records a discussion by a group of students (perhaps based upon a common set of questions about light) and then listens to the recording, which perhaps lasts for fifteen minutes or more. Transcribing all of this would take two hours or even longer, and they are busy teachers, so each listens to her recording, making an inventory of what it contains, adding numbers from the tape-recorder's counting device to make it easy to find any part again. In listening and making the inventory the teacher is looking for examples that will show the students' preconceptions about light and especially any idiosyncratic ways of thinking that may impede future learning. (The inventory can be annotated to indicate the issue for discussion that might arise from different sections of the students' talk.) Either at this point or after sharing with the other two, each of the teacher-presenters will transcribe several short sections which seem most likely to provoke useful discussion when shared with other teachers. Sometimes three well-chosen passages, perhaps of no more than twenty utterances each, support enough discussion for a two hour meeting, so the transcription of long sections is not necessary. However, it is wise to have extra material in hand, in case some sections are not so successful in provoking discussion as had been expected.

For the purposes of a group such as this, more care is needed with transcription than for the more informal monitoring discussed in the last section. Uncertain passages may need to be listened to several times: our experience is that even after dozens of hearings it is still possible for an uncertain passage suddenly to become comprehensible. However, when initially transcribing, any passage that remains uncertain should be marked, for example by enclosure in square brackets []. It is useful also to adopt some convention for representing pauses within one person's speech; for example, the length of a row of dots can show longer or shorter pauses. It is important to represent exactly what is said, including repetitions, grammatical and other confusions, and changes of direction in mid-sentence, since any of these may provide evidence about the ebb and flow of the speakers' thoughts. Two opinions are possible about the representation of dialect forms by adopting unconventional spelling: this can be seen either as an honest attempt to record exactly what occurred or as a patronizing device to show other people's speech as *strange* (with the flattering implication that one's own speech is *normal*). We return to this issue in the next section.

If possible the presenters will next meet to hear parts of one another's tapes, particularly those which seem likely to be useful and will decide which pieces they will share with other members of the group. They will also give preliminary thought to what issues might be discussed, perhaps framing questions as a way of posing the issues that seem implicit in the chosen examples, though the group of teachers may choose to pursue alternative lines of thought that may prove equally valuable.

If time is available, perhaps because the group is led by an advisory teacher or a course tutor, it is extremely helpful to send out reminders about meetings, including with them a set of notes on the previous meeting. These can either be written by the group leader or by a series of volunteers from the group. Such notes help to remind participating teachers of the point reached in the discussion, and help absentees remain part of the group. The reports make it more likely that the discussions will be cumulative rather than repetitive. If they are collected later they may provide an informal archive of the ideas put forward during the life of the group.

While the primary purpose of the kind of activities we have described is for the teachers to educate themselves in understanding the role of talk in learning, there may be occasions when a successful group is invited, or even required, to make a report to other teachers. A school which has made time and resources available for in-service study may expect feedback to be given to other members of the teaching staff. A curriculum development project may arrange a conference for representatives of its working parties, asking some of them to present *work in progress* to inform other groups and perhaps provide a model of how to go about inquiry. Slots may be made available at the conference of a professional association for members engaged in informal inquiries to share their insights and experiences. To respond to such an invitation requires not only a higher technical standard of recording and transcription, but—more importantly—requires members of the group to make far more explicit to themselves what they have learned from the activity. Preparation of a report, however informal, necessarily requires a critical survey of the examples collected and discussed, and further clarification of what each of them can reasonably be held to *show* as a basis for deciding which can be presented to a wider audience. Indeed, the presentation and discussion of examples (perhaps in a manner similar to that adopted in Chapters 2 and 3) would probably be the most important element in a report. Though making a report of this kind may provide a disturbing challenge to some teachers not used to public presentations, it often lifts the level of discussion in the group of teachers and makes the whole inquiry even more worthwhile. At the end of taught in-service professional development courses, the requirement to write a paper about what has been learned from the exercise can similarly raise the level of thinking.

However, it is important to emphasize that what we have in mind is not necessarily anything that could be described as *findings*

in the sense that some scientific researchers use the word. What we
recommend is critical reflection on material from classroom events,
reflection deepened and extended by sharing with other teachers. In
the quickly changing world of the classroom, it is seldom possible
for long to be an observer as well as a central participant; observation and reflection are luxuries that teachers usually have to forego.
But audio and video recorders have now made it possible to first
teach and then observe the same class, and what we are proposing
are ways of enhancing the professional learning that this technology
makes available to all teachers. The aim of these activities is for
teachers to achieve principled understanding, supported by illus-
trations and explanations, not *proof*, which even in formal educational research is frequently a chimera.

The questions put for discussion at a meeting would usually be
a few informal invitations to colleagues to listen to the extracts and
reflect aloud on what could be gained from them. The tutor of a
course, on the other hand, may wish to focus adult students' attention more sharply. The teachers who made the recordings mentioned above, first of groups of students and then of themselves interacting with them, were asked to record the two contexts in the
expectation that the contrast between them would throw light both
on student talk for learning and the influence of teaching upon it.
The questions given to the teachers in this case were much more
detailed, since they were intended to enable the teachers, who had
not yet met their tutor, to work on their recordings before the
course began.

Two sets of questions for discussing your tape recordings are
suggested here—one for students alone and one for students with
the teacher.

Students Alone

1. Did the students seem to learn from talking together?
2. What strategies did they use in approaching the task? Which
   were profitable? Which were not?
3. Were they able to work together? What signs of collaboration
   were there? Was there anything you might do in future to improve this?
4. Was their talk predominantly exploratory or presentational?
   [See p. 85 of this book for an explanation of these terms.]
5. Was the task a useful one for group discussion? How could it
   have been improved?
6. What problems did they experience? Were these inevitable?

Students with Teacher

1. How did the students' account of their discussion match with the discussion itself (i.e., in the recording)?

2. Did they talk to you as fully and explicitly as to one another? If not, why not?

3. Did the questions you asked prove to be appropriate and helpful? What problems did you find in eliciting the substance of their discussion?

4. What strategies did you use to improve and extend their understanding? Which were more successful and which less? Are there other strategies that you might have used?

5. What is there to be learned from comparing the student-led discussion with the discussion that you led?

Of course, it is not necessary to compare student-led talk with teacher-led talk; that had merely been chosen as a focus for that particular course. The above questions were for private consideration by the teachers concerned, whereas (as we have indicated) when teachers are to discuss material together rather different questions would be chosen to provoke discussion.

It has already been suggested that the sampling of classroom talk, including the talk of students in small groups, can be a valuable part of school-based curriculum evaluation. In the evaluation of any curriculum that has a required element of group discussion by students, valuable information could be gained by following a few groups throughout their experience of the new curriculum or by sampling their discussions at different stages of it. The possession of such material would eventually give substance and focus to staff discussions about the progress and value of the innovation. Many of the procedures outlined above would be appropriate to an evaluation of this kind, but an outside evaluator would need to anticipate and avoid difficulties that might arise if teachers came to feel that they were being criticized. Some teachers would be happy to take on the role of detached observer of their own classes, but others might feel under pressure to present only *good work*, thus changing radically the nature of their participation and making it unlikely that they would join in reflective discussion of the kind we have recommended. The control of an eventual report, spoken or written, might take high priority in participants' thoughts, and their relationships with any outside visitor playing the role of unbiased expert observer could become problematic. Though it is potentially highly valuable to record talk for the purposes of curriculum evaluation, anyone planning this would need to consider in advance how such issues could be met.

An interesting variation on the modes of working we have been describing comes when researchers team up with teachers to design and monitor new teaching practices. Brown et al. (1993), working from the School of Education at the University of California, Berkeley, attempted to foster and study the development of teaching practices in fifth through seventh grade classrooms in inner-city schools. These researchers drew on collaborative learning in two forms—reciprocal teaching (see p. 125) and the jigsaw method (which we discussed in Chapter 4)—to foster classroom communities of learning. Researchers and teachers developed a series of "design experiments" (204) centred primarily on ten week "research cycles" (197) in which students formed small groups to study and reciprocally teach the sub-topics of a major research theme undertaken by all the class. Brown et al suggest that the collaboration between "teacher-researchers" and "researcher-teachers" proved mutually beneficial. Just as with the discussions among the students, "ideas that emerge in the discourse" between teachers and researchers led to "appreciably altered understandings" (p.204) for the professional participants in the program.

We must be the first to acknowledge that participating in such a project brings additional work for a teacher. However, the benefits of teacher-researcher collaboration include, for the teacher, access to data on her own classroom, her own students, her own teaching—without having to make recordings and transcripts herself, because the research team takes care of that.

This kind of collaboration may document some outstanding work by students as teacher and researchers work together to develop a collaborative classroom. The moving discussions about war in a small literature study group in a class of third graders in a school in Tucson (Moll et al. 1993) are available not only to their own teacher, but also to the wider community of teachers and researchers precisely because these discussions were documented by a researcher. A teacher working alone would probably not have been able to take on the task of tape recording, transcribing, and analyzing the discussions of this small group which went on over a six-week period. Over that time the students read a number of novels that represented war in different ways, an "emotional and intellectual experience" (158) that led to some marked shifts in their thinking, as they themselves noted at the end of their work:

Trevor: I've changed my thoughts about war. I used to like to play war, but now it makes me sick.

Travis: I felt the same way as Trevor did. . . . Now I just don't play that way any more because I think it's so gross, after I read those books.

Aaron: I did both [play with toy soldiers and act out war games] but when I was reading the books, I didn't play with them that much.

These comments came in a final discussion in which the group met with their teacher to bring their small group work to a close. Holding such discussions and talking about their outcomes with colleagues is another means of professional development for teachers using small group work. Teachers can learn not only with fellow teachers and researchers, but also with their students.

In the next section of this chapter we consider the rather different demands—and possibilities—that arise when studying group talk as part of the work done for a higher degree.

Researching Communication and Learning for a Higher Degree

Some of our readers may intend to conduct research on group talk as part of the work required for a higher degree, whether at the master's or doctoral level. This takes questions of research design and data collection into rather more formal territory than the professional development purposes which we have discussed so far.

It is not our intention in this section to replicate other sources of advice. Whether working for a postgraduate qualification on a part-time basis while meeting the demands of a busy professional life, or whether studying full-time at the outset of a career in education, all graduate students will want to range through existing sources on the design of educational research alongside the similarly extensive literature giving guidance on planning, conducting, and writing a thesis or dissertation. Consulting tutors and supervisors is of utmost importance, and they should always be the first port of call. In this section we aim only to explore some issues that relate to post-graduate research from the specific standpoint of studying talking and learning in small groups.

One of the first issues to be clarified is whether the research is being conducted as action research (for instance by a teacher who already has a role in the setting in which research will be conducted) or whether the setting is one in which the graduate researcher normally plays no part. Some of the consequences of such different starting positions relate to practical matters such as the nature of the procedures that need to be gone through to negotiate access—clearly rather different for an outsider than for someone already teaching in the research setting.

However, such differences of starting point also pose questions to the researcher of a more fundamental nature. A practitioner, and only a practitioner, can conduct practice research: research that answers the questions that seem important from a practitioner's point of view. Such questions will relate to areas which the teacher-researcher is already engaged in, in some way, perhaps to problems for which no ready solution is otherwise seen, perhaps to nascent ideas about potential new ways of designing teaching and learning. For action research (Nixon 1981) or critical research (Carr and Kemmiss 1986) to satisfy the requirements of graduate research committees and examiners, it will need to be designed so as to generate knowledge that has illuminative power beyond the context in which it was conducted. By contrast, the outsider may have difficulty in generating questions that are practicably researchable in the classroom. Either researcher would have to make a decision about whether to conduct the research as a non-participant or as a participant observer.

An outsider will need to be certain that existing teaching practices in the school(s) selected for data collection include sufficient use of small groups to provide adequate data over the time period available for data collection. Sarah Delamont (1984), reflecting on the doctoral research she conducted which was later published as *Interaction in the Classroom,* noted in retrospect that:

> It was not possible to do anything but sit silently in most lessons, because that is what the girls did. The classes at St Luke's were silent, or had one person talking at a time.

In our own study we had initially hoped to tape record small group work that occurred *naturally.* We had in advance identified teachers who said that they used group work regularly and who were happy to call us in to record group discussions as they occurred. However, in practice we found at that time that few teachers were using any substantial amount of group work. In quantitative terms this may have changed little. A recent discussion of a study of school teachers in one region of the United Kingdom notes few teachers using cooperative group work in any serious way and few schools formally focusing on it in their curriculum policies (Ruddock 1991, 45). This finding tallies with a study in the United States (Schmuck and Schmuck 1990, cited Von Dras 1993, 59) in which only ten out of one hundred and nineteen classes observed showed student-to-student talk.

If we had only recorded group work that occurred *naturally* in the classroom we would have waited a long time to record a very small number of group discussions. Instead, we worked with the teachers to identify points in forthcoming teaching where they felt that small group discussion would be appropriate and useful. We then worked with the teachers on the design of the small group discussion tasks. When the appointed time came for this, we withdrew small groups of students from the classroom and recorded them discussing—in a small room—the task which the rest of their peers would also be addressing in the classroom. In this way we ensured (a) that we had a sufficient volume and variety of tape recorded group discussions to support meaningful analysis, (b) that we had good quality sound on the recordings for transcription purposes, (c) that the tasks which the students addressed were meaningful to them and integrated into their ongoing class work, and (d) that we caused minimum disruption to ongoing classroom teaching. It could be argued that in withdrawing our students from the classroom in order to record them we were creating an artificial and special situation. However, our aim was not to conduct a naturalistic study of the place of small group work in classrooms but to study learning talk in small groups. For this research purpose we needed an audible corpus of group talk.

We have no reason to regret this research design decision. On the contrary, we feel that it was partly the *specialness* of the situation that elicited such good efforts from the students. The talk they produced was, as has been seen, largely of a high standard in that they succeeded in coping collaboratively with rather taxing cognitive and social demands. Certainly their teachers were impressed at the quality of their talk, and some said to us that nothing like this was said in class.

As an action researcher or participant observer one has the chance to design small group discussions into regular teaching practices, so that they become part of the normal day's work. However, here the kinds of expectations which students—and teachers—attribute to teachers will apply not only to a teacher in the role of observer but also to the participation of a non-teacher observer.

It may be hard for the teacher-as-researcher to abandon familiar routines for controlling talk in classrooms. Jean Ruddock (1991) cites data collected by Denscombe (1980) in which pupils used the flexibility of a humanities curriculum development project to engage in what the teachers present thought was general chat rather than purposive learning talk, with the effect that teachers soon "were using familiar control questions to initiate conversation within the small groups" (Ruddock, 60). Ruddock (1991) documents two memorable comments made by students from her own work with Lawrence Stenhouse on the Humanities Curriculum Project. In

the first, a student articulates the difficulty of adjusting to independent group discussion in the context of everyday classroom experience that conveys quite different messages about the worth of what
students have to say:

> All our life we have been in schools. We've been taught that what
> the teacher says is right. But when we're in this room doing dis-
> cussion, it's hard for us to disagree with him after all these years.
> We sort of come to confirm with them. (62)

The other example she gives documents a pupil's insight into the
differential dynamics of student talk in a group in which the researcher acted as neutral chair and talk among students themselves:

Jim: Miss is talking too much and getting interested in the group. As
chairman she shouldn't talk, you know, as much, leaving it to the group
to argue between themselves. Well, not sort of argue—to talk between
themselves and have more discussion between themselves than with the
teacher. Because you are, you know, sort of being the chairman and not
the teacher.

[. . . . four further utterances follow . . . .]

Jim: Oi, you lot, instead of talking to Miss, talk between us lot. Everything
you say, you say to Miss. Why not talk between us lot? (64)

Our point here is not a simple empiricist one that assumes there is
a pre-existing classroom reality which researcher-observers should
try not to affect. Rather we would argue that various effects are inevitable and that graduate researchers studying small groups will
need not only to be aware of them but will also need to accommodate them into research design. Leaving a small group of students
to talk alone for a while in theory ensures a body of pupil-pupil
talk without teacher intervention. In practice some students may
find it difficult to work confidently in these circumstances, while
others may happily participate in social chitchat but not in purposive learning talk. The teacher may prefer not to leave some groups
alone at all.

This leads us to two points which a researcher will need to address at the planning stage of research on small group discussions.
These are (a) that the students may need help in learning how to
work collaboratively—if it is less familiar to them than the researcher hopes and (b) that the teacher(s) in whose classroom(s)
the research is conducted will need to make sure students realize
that small group work and what students have to say is valued.
Our discussion in Chapter 4 on implementing small group work is
relevant here.

Underlying Assumptions

The starting point as external observer or a participant in the research setting may be one over which a graduate studies researcher may have little choice. The study will need to be designed to make the best use of the opportunities which either role might bring. However, the assumptions which will underline the study are very much within the researcher's control. These are not always reflected upon and may be taken for granted. In our experience practitioners working as researchers may be fairly comfortable with the practical aspects of their research but less happy to address issues that they think of as theoretical or academic. What this stance overlooks is that theoretical assumptions of some kind always influence research design and the choice of research method. Even if the researcher leaves these assumptions implicit, they will be clear to supervisors and examiners who may query their appropriateness or the extent to which data collection decisions are consistent with them. Another issue is that problems can arise later on in the study if it turns out that the data collection or analysis options followed provide little basis for significant commentary on the study's research questions. Theory and method are linked in research design in a number of complex ways, and it is always helpful to integrate the two. For this reason, we should like to give some examples of different assumptions that may be brought to the study of talk in small learning groups. This is an illustrative not an inclusive discussion—that would take a book in its own right—and it will be more helpful if considered in conjunction with our theoretical commentary in Chapter 6.

The first of these is the most basic and concerns the researcher's idea about what learning is. We discussed competing views in Chapter 1 and will not repeat that argument here. But a view of learning as constructing knowledge will lead to different research questions and the use of different methodologies from those that follow from a view of learning as transmission, recall, or comprehension of authoritative information. Research design in the latter case is likely to follow an input-output model and to use tests of accuracy and of individual recall as a measure of the success of the groups. If the talk itself is examined at all, it may be only from the standpoint of checking when some of these formulations arose.

A second concerns the goals toward which it is assumed small group talk should be addressed. Are the students to develop their own purposes, or is it assumed that group talk should be oriented to the teacher's instructional goals? For instance, Brown and Palincsar's (1989) *reciprocal teaching* used four pre-structured activities of questioning, clarifying, summarizing, and predicting to support group discussion "because they are excellent comprehension-monitoring devices" (Brown et al. 1993, 195–6). Brown et al. see the purpose of reciprocal teaching as "everyone [..] trying to arrive at consensus concerning meaning, relevance, and importance" (196) led by the adult teacher's "clear instructional goal" of "keeping the discussion focused on the content and seeing that enough discussion takes place to ensure a reasonable level of understanding" (205). This study used clinical interviews which posed thought experiments to students to track their retention of knowledge and the extent to which it could be applied.

In Brown et al.'s (1993) use of the jigsaw method: "Teachers and researchers construct goals for what they want each research group to accomplish" (205). Use of the jigsaw model aims to develop expertise among student groups in different sub-areas of a topic— which these groups of students then teach to others. The *jigsaw* metaphor indicates a view of pre-existing knowledge which can be broken down into constituent parts and then re-assembled back into a whole, with groups sharing the workload of re-assembly. Within such frameworks analysis of group talk will be led by measures which track the gradual formation of consensus and which judge the success of the group work by the extent to which it meets pre-existing instructional goals. In turn, the need to provide data from which to construct those measures will drive the strategy for data collection and analysis.

Two competing assumptions are whether we view learning as something accomplished by an individual alone or as something that is accomplished jointly with other people. The second of these assumptions is a special kind of constructivist view of knowledge, social constructivism, which has led to the development of the growing field of social cognition (Resnick et al. 1991).

If we think of learning as something that is accomplished alone then we are likely to design studies of small group work which examine the effects of participation in small group discussion on individual performance on chosen parameters. James Wertsch (1991) has commented on what he sees as "the tendency of psychological research, especially in the United States, to examine human mental functioning as if it exists in a cultural, institutional and historical vacuum" (2). He goes on to cite Barbara Rogoff who adds that this "emphasis on the individual [...] has also been characteristic of the incorporation of Piaget's theory into American research in the modern era" (Rogoff 1990, 4, cited Wertsch 1991, 3). Despite the strong conceptual hold which Piaget's idea of knowledge as personally (i.e., individually) constructed has exerted over decades of developmental research, Resnick (1991) points out that nevertheless, constructivism ultimately forces researchers to "treat social processes as cognition" (2) because "our daily lives are filled with instances in which we influence each other's constructive processes by providing information, pointing things out to one another, asking questions, and arguing with and elaborating on each other's ideas" (2).

The study we have presented in this book gives many examples of the kinds of questions a researcher might want to pursue from a standpoint that sees knowledge as socially constructed. However, the kinds of questions we have asked of our data are by no means the only ones that could be asked. One of our interests was to look at the social knowledge brought in to the classroom by students themselves. Salman and Claire (1984) examined the frames of reference which both teachers and students brought into the collaborative classroom. A view of knowledge as socially shared can profitably bring participants from outside the classroom into the research framework as, for instance, in Moll and Greenberg's (1990) study of the role of household *funds of knowledge* in classroom learning. To study this, the researchers had to incorporate into their research strategy the collection of ethnographic data on those households so they could subsequently track the contribution of these household funds of knowledge to the classroom learning of the students in this study.

The same prior assumption could also lead to investigations of the effects of social factors on the cognitive performance of individuals. Perret-Clermont, Perret, and Bell (1991) describe conducting just such a series of studies of the effects of social interaction on the cognitive development of individuals, designed within the classic paradigm of pre-test, experimental session, and post-test. The tests were of students' performance on Piagetian conservation tasks or on Piagetian tasks relating to the representation of social relations; the interactions in the experimental sessions with peers and adults were varied to provide a number of experimental conditions. The results led the researchers to question their initial theoretical starting point: rather than social interactions being readily identifiable as causal factors productive of different forms of cognitive activity, interactions were used by subjects as a ways "to give meaning to the persons and tasks with which they were interacting" (p.43). In a second phase of studies the researchers shifted their unit of analysis from the individual to the social interaction itself. As a result of conducting studies with this different focus they developed the view that the individual's thinking is not at all independent of social settings and interpersonal relationships. The corollary they draw from this provides a salutary warning for any researcher:

> In other words, the cognitive competence of a subject can only be *seen* by someone who has the necessary cognitive and social skills to relate properly to that subject. (55)

Another assumption concerns the role we allot to the part played in developing new understanding by various tools and symbol systems. This focus has led to the idea of "distributed cognitions" (Saloman 1993) which acknowledges that not only other people but also "culturally provided tools and implements" (xiii) help to support thinking. Examples which Saloman gives of the artifacts which can be used to aid understanding range from the cards on which a student might make notes to powerful computer software used by professionals. Roy Pea (1993) in the same volume locates the conceptual basis of the idea of distributed intelligence in work on the ecology of perception (1979, 1982) which has focused on what everyday objects *afford* to their users through their design as artifacts. The *affordances* provided by the objects—a handle we can turn, a paper and pencil, a computer display—are tools that "carry intelligence in them" (1993, 53). Pea argues that we have become so accustomed to what is afforded to us by some of these objects that we no longer notice this help and treat the objects as if the reified intelligence inhering in them is all our own.

We can show the relevance of this insight for the design of research on small group talk by looking at a study of "the potential of computers as a means of promoting *exploratory* talk" in UK primary classrooms, the Spoken Language and New Technology (SLANT) Project (Fisher 1993a). Fisher notes that a shortage of computers in UK primary classrooms—despite a statutory requirement in the National Curriculum for primary students to begin to develop computing skills—has led to group (not individual) computer-based learning becoming the norm.

Among a variety of other influences on the features of the students' discourse, Fisher suggests that the design of the software they are using plays an important part. The discourse structure associated with the use of adventure games—software which was characterized as having a closed structure—was constrained by the narrow band of options for users' actions afforded by the game. Despite the stated intentions of the software manufacturer to provide support for thinking linked to school subjects, a random press of a key often gave a quicker solution than the application of wider knowledge. Strikingly, the researchers found that the "computer, in the games software, is generally the participant taking all the *complicated* decisions" (1993a, 106). Other rigidly structured software, such as mathematical problems posed within a game format, often led to similarly constrained roles for the students and similarly constrained discourse features. This study clearly demonstrates that the use of a powerful tool such as a computer does not necessarily lead to discourse which is used in varied and exploratory ways. The methodological lesson is that tools and implements used in educational settings, no less than the design of a typewriter, carry intrinsic features which may or may not be conducive to the generation of a corpus of varied, wide-ranging and exploratory pupil talk for subsequent analysis. Some schools use Quick Mail (Brown et al. 1993, 205) and access to the Internet to provide students with the opportunity for computer-based interaction with people and information sources beyond the school's physical boundaries. The influence of participation in more open computer-based interactions in the learning conducted by small groups opens up a new area of study.

Working on the Data

Recordings and transcripts that are to be used for graduate research will need to conform to more rigorous standards of preparation, transcription, and presentation of the analytical path followed. A teacher informally monitoring her own teaching may start and stop her project at will, and groups of teachers working together for professional development purposes can choose to focus on just those short structures of interaction that are of interest for their own professional learning. However, a graduate student must demonstrate that the data collection and analysis decisions made are appropriate to illuminate the research questions which the study set out to investigate and must set out the basis for the ideas formulated in the dissertation. Having designed a data collection strategy that reflects the researcher's interests in regard to age of students, school subject, type of classroom, task structure, etc., it will be important to ensure that the analytical decisions made while working on the data are clearly and logically linked to the research questions—and also that these decisions are transparent to supervisors, research committee members and external examiners, as well as to other researchers. This will entail presenting data in a way that makes the basis of analytical decisions available to others for query, comment, or critique.

Recording and transcription. Data are not data if they are unintelligible, so that an initial research design priority must be to ensure consistently high standards of recording for all the group discussions in the corpus of data. It will almost certainly be necessary to record the discussions in a room off the main classroom. In a room with soft furnishings and a small class, it may just be possible to obtain transcribable recordings by using directional or neck microphones for a group working in a corner well away from the rest of the class. What will the class, as well as the group, be doing? Will there be loud noises from movements elsewhere? Just the rustlings and tappings of papers or objects being moved on the table on which a microphone is standing can be enough to make students' voices unintelligible. All of this varies greatly according to circumstances, so it will be important to conduct pilot recordings in advance of making key data collection decisions. Will you be able to tell which students are speaking? If you are using video, will you be able to ensure that none of your speakers disappears from view? Will the quality of the sound and/or vision you obtain be good enough for an outsider (supervisor or examiner) to be able to hear what you think you heard, see what you think you saw?

As we have seen, to make sense of a great deal of what goes on it is necessary to understand the context in which the students are working. You will need to document the context by making observational notes of events in class teaching related to the group work, keeping a record of the different tasks used and of details relating to each taping (students' names, task, venue, starting and stopping time, tape identification code, your notes taken at the time about background circumstances, perhaps photographs of students, task setting or equipment), and maintaining a cumulative research diary. You may need to supplement the recordings of group work with interviews with teachers and students to gain the background information you need.

The number of groups you record and the length of the discussions you record in total will depend primarily on your own research questions, but also on features of the classrooms and the teaching to which you have access. If your interest is in students new to group discussion you will need to record a number of different groups that are all at the start up stage. If you are interested in the way group discussion relates to a particular teaching cycle, you may want to follow all the subgroups in one class—recording them in turn— over the period of time it takes to complete that teaching cycle. If you are interested in tracing the development of small group discussion skills you may want to track a small number of groups from the first occasion when they work together through to their achievement of sophisticated expertise with this mode of working.

Whatever your focus of interest you will need to bear in mind the time it takes to transcribe and analyze recordings of group talk.

We found that a reliable transcription of informal talk from a well-recorded tape could require from eight to twelve times the running time of the recording. This is for transcription alone. It allows for preparing transcriptions that use pre-defined conventions to show the lengths of pauses, longer silences, and overlaps between speakers and to note revolution counter numbers at different points so as to be able to locate sections of discourse. For our original analytical purposes we presented our conversations on paper like the script of a play with speakers' (anonymous) names to the left and utterances to the right. We used lengths of pauses to help decide where an utterance began and ended, showing short pauses (as for an intake of breath) as a comma, and pauses of longer duration that were nevertheless too short to measure on the tape recorder's revolution counter, by three dots. Pauses of longer duration were shown by revolution counter numbers. (This level of detail is invaluable for analytical purposes but is less interesting for a reader so we have edited some of this information out of the transcriptions quoted in this book.)

Other conventions may be drawn on to represent interactional features and stresses. See, for example, the appendix on transcription conventions in Deborah Tannen's 1989 study of the literary strategies embodied in ordinary conversation. In our original research we thought it was important not to edit out the informal and dialect features of the speech of the students we recorded and we devised a number of non-standard spellings which we hoped would faithfully represent them. Working on the transcripts again during the preparation of this book we felt less happy with this strategy and decided to re-represent their speech in standard spelling. Tannen (1989) cites the work of Preston (1982 and 1985) suggesting that transcription through non-standard spellings is rarely consistent. She also notes that the use of non-standard spellings produces negative impressions of the speaker in readers and so misrepresents speakers—in that the casual pronunciations represented via non-standard spellings actually may be standard in speech.

We used a judgment about the length of an utterance to block out chunks of speech against speakers' names; this means that the left hand columns of our transcripts look like short blocks of prose. Deborah Tannen, whose focus of analysis made intonation very important, presents examples "in poetic lines rather than prosaic blocks" (202). She uses intonation units (a researcher should budget additional time to transcribe these) to capture the rhythms within each utterance and then represents these rhythms in the layout of the text. These transcripts proceed line by line where the parameters of each line represent sections of an utterance.

By contrast, Fisher (1993a and b) and her colleagues were interested in features relating to whole sections of talk, because they wanted to see whether features of students' discourse in small groups were related to features of the computer software which the students were using. Because they were interested in work at the computer, these groups had to be video-recorded and the transcription task included noting not only students' actions (such as key pressing or reading from the screen) but also "the computer's input to the discourse" (Fisher 1993a, 101). The length of those recordings was indicated by the length of the group's activity sessions on the computer which usually lasted more than half an hour and could be up to one hour in length. Activity sessions of this length quickly provide a large volume of data to transcribe and analyze; in her 1993a paper, Fisher chooses to work on discourse extracts because they are *interesting* but also notes a prior decision that any extracts chosen should be typical of at least 20 percent of that session. In this way she introduces a second sampling frame for discussion purposes, giving the reader some access to knowledge of how a selected extract relates to others not quoted.

An interest in discourse features leads to larger scale analytical categories than, for instance, those we have discussed in the research we have reported here. Whole sections of the discussion are categorized according to the underlying structure of the type of talk that is going on. We discussed earlier the *adventure game talk* which these researchers felt could be readily categorised into an "initiation/response/feedback, or follow-up" structure. Elsewhere in the materials these researchers categorized sections of talk as "cumulative text talk" (Fisher 1993b, 247) in which students take turns creating a text to be put into the computer, each accepting what the previous speaker said, "disputational talk" (Fisher 1993b, 247), where students challenge each other in turn and do not reach a resolution, and "exploratory talk" (Fisher 1993a, b), where students each contribute ideas and plans and each offering is listened to (although not necessarily agreed with).

A study with a rather different focus of interest (Bennett and Cass, 1989) categorized sections of talk into *instructional,* which could include both giving and seeking instruction, and *procedural,* which had to do with the management of the groups' work. The *instructional* category had four sub-categories of judgments, suggestions, answers, and explanations. This category system was used to support a correlational study of the effects of group composition on the interactive processes within groups and the understanding achieved in them. *Composition* was operationalized by prior measures of individual attainment sorting students into high or low achievers.

What we hope is clear from this discussion is that there are many ways of analyzing tapes, reflecting the focus of interest of the researcher. The analytical options need to be thought through in outline early in the project because they will affect both the amount of data that is needed (line by line analysis may need a smaller corpus of data than an analysis which sees whole sections of talk as units) and the transcription conventions that will be needed. In their turn, these requirements will have implications for the amount of time that will be needed to make and transcribe the recordings, even before any analysis per se begins. However, we don't see a strong dividing line between the transcription and analysis—as captured above, transcription decisions are really the first step in analysis.

Similarly, the activity chosen for the study may have its own naturalistic time parameters, and this will force certain lengths of recording time on the researcher—who may then have to make secondary sampling decisions for analytical purposes. The time budget allotted to data collection and analysis will be crucial to the project's success. All of those features will need thinking through at the start of the study. In research on group talk as in other types of research pilot work, trying out different options at the start of the study will be invaluable. We have sometimes found novice researchers hesitating about going into the field until they feel they have decided exactly what they are going to do. We would recommend making a number of small, manageable excursions into the field at the pilot stage of the work: record some groups, try out different modes of transcription, experiment with different modes of analysis, work out how long it takes you as well as checking if the transcription conventions you are using really capture the features important for your research questions.

At the same time, the courses you will be following as part of your graduate research will develop new understandings and competencies that you will be able to apply to working on your data. Tonya Dix (1993) describes how she used an assignment for a graduate course on educational measurement to help her design a grid which she used to record the observations she made of her (third, fourth, and fifth grade) students engaged in discussions of literature and also how she then developed a self-evaluation tool which the students themselves could use. Ultimately this work became a master's level curriculum development project exploring evaluation strategies for discussion of non-fiction in small groups. This reflected a shift in the focus of her study from the talk and dynamics within small groups to their curricular outcomes. In her study, success was seen as the achievement of sustained joint inquiry, producing ever more complex questions on the part of the learners.

In this chapter we have discussed some of the issues involved in studying small groups for three different purposes: informal monitoring, professional and curricular development, and in conducting a research project for a higher degree. We said at the beginning of the chapter that the purposes overlap. We hope we have shown how, far from this comment being simply one about the boundaries of our categories, it is rather the case that teachers' purposes may overlap in these different ways of working. Work conducted or begun in one mode may lead to useful spin-offs for another. The different audiences in each case, however, suggest different levels of formality of study design, data collection, and analysis.

Finally, we should emphasize that we do not see any one of these modes as being intrinsically of more value than another. Any of them may lead to valuable insights and new understandings of the links between communicating and learning in small groups. We hope some of our readers will try out for themselves one or more of these ways of studying group talk.

Chapter Six

Making Meaning Through Talk

Our original study was led by two guiding ideas. As set out in Chapter 1 we had a view of learning as something accomplished jointly with other people. Along with this emphasis on its social nature, we saw learning as the reshaping—perhaps radical reshaping—of ways of seeing the world. In our research, therefore, we looked not at individuals but at groups. And we looked at groups working on learning tasks which required that they consider and develop new frameworks of meaning rather than memorizing or reproducing existing forms offered by a teacher.

In Chapters 2 and 3 we have given extracts from our data which demonstrate the inner workings of the link between communication and learning, showing the means from which collaboration is made in small group talk and illustrating some of the cognitive purposes to which it is addressed. Our guiding assumptions were, in the event, well-supported by our data, and they are at the core of the advice on the implementation of small group learning which we have set out in Chapter 4.

The crucial import of these two ideas is that small group work as we have set it out here is a way of changing learners through changing how they learn. This transformative potential of learning in small groups derives from the opportunities which conversations between peers, particularly discussions oriented towards learning, provide for the generation by learners of new ideas, new insights and more complex points of view.

In this chapter we want to explore the basis for these transformations of meaning which dialogue with others can achieve. To do this we draw in part on our original analyses: of the construction of understanding through the cyclical interplay of viewpoints and of the role of questions, hypothetical statements, and answers in the shaping of joint inquiry.

We then go on to draw out the significance of this analysis from the theoretical standpoint of dialogism. When we carried out our study we characterized the talk we recorded as dialogue, and we developed a model for understanding learning conversations that captured features which we saw as characteristic of dialogic speech. There are many points of resonance between what we set out then and Bakhtin's work (1981), published in English since we conducted our research. This provides an apt theoretical framework to reconsider the model we developed—and we will use it to clarify what we wrote before.

Learning and Development

Before moving on we should like to consider the relationship between learning and development and to emphasize the importance of other people in promoting development. We begin with the idea of development. Initially we had based the design (Barnes and Todd 1977, 1–4) of our original study on a view of development that was strongly influenced by the "stage" theory of the Piagetian model (Piaget 1950, 1965). We assumed that the thinking of thirteen-year-olds of average ability would be mainly at the intuitive level of concrete operations, rising occasionally under especially helpful conditions to the hypothetico-deductive thinking of formal operations. What might these conditions be? We assumed that one way of achieving hypothetico-deductive thinking would be through internalizing the viewpoints of other people, and that this internalization would take place in the course of dialogues in which different viewpoints would be inter-related through verbal interaction with other people. Our original hope was to be able to trace the strategies that encouraged or discouraged hypothetico-deductive thinking. We had even hoped to assign each utterance to a cognitive level, according to an analytical scheme to be based on the developmental sequence set out in the Piagetian model.

Social and cultural factors play little part in the Piagetian model of cognitive development which sees intelligence developing out of the child's interpretation of his actions on the world. We should pause here and draw attention to three key features of this model of development: its notion of pre-fixed cognitive stages; the importance attributed to the individual child's own actions as the impetus for transition through these stages via the development of new interpretive schemas; and the intrinsically hierarchical view of a series of different cognitive levels. The achievement of the use of logically formal operations and the capacity to be reflexive about one's own thinking are seen as the pinnacle of the developmental process. Development from this standpoint is the cumulative and serial attainment by an individual of these different cognitive levels.

Our idea of the destination of development—the achievement of formal operations—came from the mainstream of this model. However, we took the idea that appreciation of alternative perspectives might be aided through interaction with others from Piaget's work on the development of moral judgment (Piaget 1965) and in part from his early work on language and thought in the child (Piaget 1960). Here other individuals are admitted to the model in a positive way, and this was at the heart of our research design which also drew, without being explicit about the differences between them, on the rather different model of development set out by Vygotsky.

At the time we perhaps glossed over an inconsistency in the Piagetian model about the role of social factors in learning. We have already cited in Chapter 5 Lauren Resnick's comment that the personally-constructivist model developed by Piaget inevitably leads, at some point, to the adoption of social constructivism—precisely because individuals do not live or grow up alone. It is not possible to experience the world solely through one's own actions because our actions are mediated through the social setting we inhabit. Even the artifacts we manipulate carry meanings and intelligence from the society and culture which made them.

In Vygotsky's (1978) discussion of Piaget's research on the language and thought of the child (Piaget 1960) he notes that Piaget's observations had prompted Piaget to:

> conclude that communication produces the need for checking and confirming thoughts, a process that is characteristic of adult thought. (90)

Vygotsky added that Piaget had "shown that cooperation provides the basis for a child's moral judgment" (90).

The essence of Vygotsky's point here is that things that are learned in the social sphere later become internalized. Language is first used for communication with others, but these social encounters with others produce the need to check and confirm thoughts. This process then provides the basis for new modes of internal mental functioning. In this way social experiences affect the course of individual development.

Vygotsky's emphasis on the importance of the other, like that of Mead (1974) suggests that our consciousness develops out of taking the same relation toward ourselves as others have to us (Vygotsky 1981, cited Kozulin 1992, xxiv). In young students this may occur through imitation, either of other students or of adults. However, in older students or adults one would expect to find this awareness of self from the perspective of the other developed in a variety of complex ways in the course of interaction.

Here it is important to pull out some essential features of Vygotsky's model of development. It is a model which is quintessentially social: behaviors and operations appear first in the social sphere with others and only then become available to support the individual's internal mental functioning. Rather than a steady progress through pre-fixed stages, development proceeds through upheavals and revolutions as different functions mature at each individual's own rate. The destination of the developmental process is not some finite stopping point at which we can say development is completed. Rather it is to become human: to master, on the one hand, the surrounding environment through the use of tools and on the other, oneself by the use of signs that have personal social and cultural meaning. The implications of this model are that this process is never completed. While adults achieve higher (more abstract) forms of mental functioning than young students, earlier forms of thought may remain buried within apparently completed developmental processes. Development, then, means not only to become, but to remain, fully human among other humans.

This conception of development led Vygotsky to distinguish between learning and development—a distinction which may at first sight seem difficult to come to terms with. In everyday educational discourse we use the word learning to refer both to what Vygotsky meant by learning and to what he meant by development. For Vygotsky the development which learning supports takes us towards the higher cultural functions which he saw as specifically human. It is a powerful distinction which helps to explain the phenomenon of learners suddenly and apparently unpredictably manifesting judgment, deliberation, and choice over difficult issues. Learning drags development behind it but then development overlaps learning to reach new developmental terrain. Vygotsky thought of the things we can already do as past history. Of far greater importance is the developmental level we might achieve with others in socially mediated activity which he characterized as the zone of proximal development (Vygotsky 1978, 84–91). The essential feature "of learning is that it creates the zone of proximal development" (90)—a point of awakening of internal developmental processes. The rationale of learning, then, in terms of the individual's development, is not the grasping of the meaning of a word, or the achievement of an arithmetical operation such as multiplication or division or even the mastery of writing, but rather the more complex internal development processes in thinking which are awakened (made proximal) by the mastering of these operations. These

> are able to operate only when the child is interacting with people in his environment and in cooperation with his peers. (90

School learning provides one familiar setting for the awakening of these internal intellectual processes. Indeed, Vygotsky described school subjects as an "internal subterranean developmental network" (1978, 91). However, his criticism of educational systems is that the design of school learning experiences can be led by the custom of testing the learning that has already been achieved "orient[ing] learning towards yesterday's development" (1978, 89) instead of designing experiences to support the developmental processes which a learner is only just beginning at the point of initial operational achievement.

The recordings we made provide the opportunity, as we have seen, to observe students "interacting with people in their environment and cooperating with their peers"—in effect, to observe the creation of zones of proximal development. We want to examine next some of the features we found in the students' communication through which we think this awakening of internal development is enacted.

The Nature of Conversation and Meaning

As co-researchers our method of trying jointly to understand our data was in some ways not dissimilar to the paths followed by the groups recorded. For instance, we read what other scholars had written about analyzing linguistic data; we developed and practiced the analytical approaches which derived from these writings; we applied these approaches to the group talk we were studying—and then we got stuck for a while because the techniques we were trying to use were not adequate to capture the complexity and fluidity of live learning talk. We worked our way out of this problem by trying out a series of different formulations on the data, none of which was adequate in itself but out of which we ultimately put different elements together to develop a new framework.

The original methods we had tried, drawn from linguistic analysis, had conceived of meaning as something relatively fixed and fairly well-locatable in single utterances. But we soon encountered two particular difficulties. On the one hand we found that a great deal might be going on in just one utterance; several equally important things often seemed to be going on at the same time. So it was not at all possible to put utterances into categories on a one-to-one basis, because some utterances belonged in several categories. On the other hand it also seemed that the meanings for what was going on in the conversations were constructed not from any one utterance on its own but from cycles of utterances, perhaps over quite lengthy sections of interaction. The cycles we found, were not readily isolable. They adhered to the interrelationships between utterances and to the participants' intentions for and interpretations of these utterances.

The analytical problems we had stumbled on are well expressed in Todorov's 1983 summary of what he thinks of as the "obvious" distinction between language and discourse. Language is an abstract system from which, using the input of the lexicon and grammatical rules, sentences can be produced as output. Discourse is the concrete manifestation of this abstract system. Discourses are produced in a specific context of time, place, persons present, and their relationships to each other. Speakers combine these circumstances with the linguistic elements of language to produce—not sentences which actually noone utters—but utterances.

Todorov reminds us that meaning does not arrive in the same way in language and in discourse. In contrast to the single meaning of words and sentences that are not part of a context, utterances can be interpreted—and used—in any number of different ways. They not only have one direct meaning but many potential indirect meanings. These arise from the interpretations that may be attributed to an utterance in context. Bakhtin, whose ideas we will consider in more detail at the end of this chapter, also distinguishes between "the *sentence* as a *unit of language*, as distinct from the *utterance* as a unit of speech communication" (Bakhtin 1986, 73).

Such situated meanings may be indirect but Todorov (1983) emphasizes that they are by no means marginal:

> Indirect production of meaning is present in all discourse, and in some kinds of discourse, including some important ones, it is probably wholly dominant—for example in everyday conversation, or in literature. (12)

The linguistic tradition which we had initially turned to for the development of an analytical scheme admits only direct, literal meaning to analysis. Todorov argues that "linguists deny symbolic meaning by non-recognition and lack of attention" (p.14), exclusions which are justified on empiricist principles of counting only what can be perceived.

Our own conclusions, based on analysis of our data, diverged sharply from the general linguistical formulae which we had used for our starting point. We found that meaning is indeterminate and open to change, that it is dependent on context, and that it is spread over exchanges of utterances rather than inhering in any one of them. This latter point entails that meaning is not something owned by one participant in a discussion but something that, developing and changing as it does in the course of a series of contributions by different participants, is constructed and reconstructed by all of them.

We realized that meaning arises from the tacit knowledge which participants use to attribute meaning to what is said. Differing participants bring different bodies of knowledge to the discussion and at different moments in the discussion treat one or another element of these bodies of knowledge as relevant to understanding what is said. These bodies of knowledge, and elements of them, are not static but are affected by what is going on in the discussion as well as by participants' evaluations of what is going on. In this way, participants use ever-changing frames of reference to assign meaning and relevance to their own and other people's utterances. However, although ever-changing, these frames of reference remain attuned to the context of what has gone before, as we shall discuss later.

We can illustrate the importance of context in the attribution of meaning by giving an extract from one of the dialogues we recorded. Without the aid of a commentary, what sense can be made of this extract?

> "It's like a diving, diving suit isn't it?"
> "Yes . . . it's full of air"
> "It's only full of air so he can breathe"
> "No it, it keeps, it stops the, er,"
> "There's so much pressure when he gets down"
> "Yes"
> "It stops, it stops it from pushing it in"

To make any sense at all of this we need to have some knowledge of deep sea diving equipment and its functions. However, this alone is not enough. We need to know something about the people who are talking and why they are doing so. Perhaps having travelled this far with us the reader will guess that the speakers here are the thirteen-year-old students in our study—but it is not immediately obvious that three different voices spoke and secondly, it is not clear what the *it* is. The students were discussing a question set by a teacher as a means of getting them to apply their knowledge of air pressure to

the issue of what would happen to a space traveller if he stepped
out into space without a space suit on. It is while they are discussing the space suit that Barry says: "It's like a diving, diving suit,
isn't it?" The reader may care now to re-read the passage in the light
of this new information, in particular asking what the pronoun *it*
refers to upon its various occurrences. We provide a parallel commentary which, however, we see as hypothetical, as less than adequate to the complex meanings available to participants, and as necessarily involving the use of our own knowledge.

35. Graham: Yes . . . it's full of air

"It" seems here to refer to the space
suit, but since being "full of air" is a
characteristic shared by the diving
suit there is a potential ambiguity
present.

36. Barry: It's only full of air so he
can breathe

The reference here is entirely ambiguous. As is normal in conversation, however, the ambiguity does
not in the least check the exchange.

37. Graham: No it, it keeps, it stops
the, er,

Graham must be attributing a meaning to Barry's "it" since he begins to
contradict the statement, but
whether he himself is referring to
space suit or diving suit remains as
indeterminate to us as to the other
two boys (unless we look at his later
attempt at No. 40).

38. Alec: There's so much pressure
when he gets down

Here we apply our knowledge retro-
spectively. "When he gets down"
must (we say) mean into the depths
of the sea, so Alec (who here speaks
for the first time) has identified the
"it" of the two preceding utterances
as the diving suit.

39. Barry: Yes

Barry now adds his support to this
identification that is gradually taking shape.

40. Graham: It stops, it stops it from
pushing it in

Graham has now abandoned "it" =
space suit and tacitly accepts the alternative identification. He also introduces a second referent for "it"
and we use our tacit knowledge to

identify this as the pressure in the depths of the sea.

41. Barry: I wonder how fish and all them survive down there then

This tacit identification is used by Barry as a springboard for a venture into a new topic.

The purpose of this analysis has been not merely to point out the way in which complex structures of tacit knowledge (both of the social context and of the matters referred to) are used with great rapidity during conversation in attributing meaning to what is said. More important, perhaps, is the observation that these meanings are fluid and indeterminate—for the participants as much as for the observer. The indeterminacy here enables the boys briefly to try out a possible relationship between space suits and diving suits before moving to another topic, and this is characteristic of how meaning develops during the flux of these learning conversations.

In the extract quoted above, the students use continually changing bodies of knowledge to interpret what is going on in the conversation. The first utterance comes from Barry, who generates it by mapping his intentions onto a set of linguistic forms which from his point of view represent them. This utterance is interpreted by Graham who, using a body of knowledge he considers relevant, assigns a meaning to the words spoken. On the basis of this interpretation of Barry's utterance, Graham replies by selecting the form of words that constitute the second utterance. That is, Graham's reply incorporates an implicit interpretation of Barry's utterance and with it an unspoken context to which it would be relevant. When Barry hears what Graham has said, he in his turn interprets the words by attributing to Graham a frame of understanding which they share. In speaking the third utterance he generates a new intention that incorporates a view of what has gone on before, a view not only of what Graham meant but also of what Graham had thought he (Barry) had meant in the first utterance. Barry and Graham engage in their exchange on the basis of a common assumption of operating in the same frame of reference, of using the same body of knowledge in understanding one another.

From an observer's point of view, replaying the conversation at leisure, it may appear that they have at times attributed intentions falsely to one another, but this itself may be misleading. The very indefiniteness of the meanings or intentions—their lack of reflective definition, that is—allows participants in discussion to collaborate in developing a thread of meaning which may change many times, and radically, in the course of talk.

Both the forms of words and the frames of knowledge are essential to meaning. Barry's words "It's only full of air so he can breathe" do not in themselves have a determinate meaning. However, unless Graham's past history has led him to assign meanings to these words which are at least similar to Barry's and Alec's, then the three cannot communicate. Todorov refers to this cooperative aspect of the interpretation of utterances as the "principle of pertinence" (1983, 29). We assume that speech is motivated; apparent incoherence leads us to seek an allusion on the speaker's part that will allow us to generate a sense for what is said.

Barry, Graham, and Alec bring their own histories to the interpretation of what goes on in their conversation, histories which themselves contain inconsistencies. Indeed, a person's history may offer several interpretative frames to select from. However, as a group they have a history too, since in the course of interaction, however brief, they are constructing common meanings. To take an extreme example, some long-standing groups generate catchphrases which for them carry implications which are closed to everyone else. But all groups in a lesser degree set up unique meanings, though they may in many cases be impermanent.

What is the status of these intentions and interpretations? Do they have an existence except in so far as the participants reconstruct them later in reflection? The very coherence of a conversational text (as interpreted by an observer) testifies to the moment by moment existence of some common understanding. However, any retrospective account would be very different from the shadowy and half-formed meanings which momentarily shape the exchange. It seems helpful therefore to distinguish *operational* meanings from *reflective* meanings.

A participant in a conversation can attend to only part of what is happening. What is going on includes his interpretation of what has already been said, both from the point of view of its content and of its implications for social relationships. In turn these interpretations depend on knowledge which he already holds of the speaker, the subject-matter, the situation, and the norms of discourse. What is going on also includes remembering what he himself has said before, scanning possible replies he might make, reading non-verbal signals (including those from participants who are not at that moment speaking), and attending to extraneous features of his environment.

Many of these may be reworked during the course of the conversation. There may be a time lag between Barry's making an utterance and Graham's responding negatively to that utterance, to the situation, to Barry's facial expression, and so on. Finally, he interprets the utterance as sarcastic and aggressive: some time later (maybe some utterances later) he responds accordingly.

In this way, throughout a conversation, participants not only speak and hear, but they also construct a cumulative and idiosyncratic account of what has been going on. This account is a construction in that many events are excluded from it, and it is made of interpretations of events, rather than the events themselves. This business of constructing an account of what happened in a conversation does not necessarily end when the talking stops and the conversers separate; it continues when participants reflect upon what was said. It may be that much of the meaning of the events is constructed like this, after the conversation is over. But even this is not fixed; the reflective meaning is always open to change because of new information available, or new insights achieved by the speaker-hearer as he reflects on events that are past, or talks about them to others.

So far we have confined our attention mainly to the content of what is said. During every conversation, however, the participants must not only operate as if they shared one another's understanding of the matter discussed, but must also negotiate how they will relate to one another in discussing it. "Negotiate" may prove a misleading metaphor, since the social meanings put forward and accepted or rejected are at least as indeterminate and ambiguous as the referential meanings so far discussed. Todorov (1983) has commented that multiple meanings are evoked by the very fact of an utterance and by its direction. Uttering something is an action, not just a means of transmitting information. An enunciation necessarily also evokes implications about the speaker and the person(s) to whom the utterance is addressed. So as well as the content of an utterance there is also this implication to be taken into account.

In order to deal with these two kinds of meaning we propose that every utterance in this type of learning conversation should be said to offer two Frames: one, the Content Frame, offers an interpretation of the subject in hand, while the other, the Interaction Frame, offers an interpretation of the social relationships which are shaping the interaction. Each of these frames is fleeting, rapidly alterable, ever-changing. We shall approach this obliquely by way of the route which we ourselves took in formulating these concepts.

Our first approaches to the analysis of small group talk were colored by our previous experience of analyzing teacher-class dialogue. By virtue of his role a teacher claims the right and responsibility of exercising control over the subject-matter of lessons and over the patterns of communication. For much of the time, most pupils accept this right and responsibility as normal. To take a real example, when a teacher in a science practical lesson asks a pupil, "And so what? What beyond that? What's this got to do with atoms?" he is enacting his right to control the direction of the talk. He is indicating that he wants the pupil to link what he has just said with ideas about atoms; moreover, he probably does not want just any ideas but particular ideas presented during an earlier lesson. At the same time he is making it clear that the pupil has no option but to attempt to answer this question: the pupil's next move is firmly laid down for him, whatever his private wishes, his role in that context being progressively defined for him.

As soon as one turns to small groups where the participants are of equal status, this is no longer the case. In the conversations we are considering, each participant tries to guide the dialogue in the direction he wishes, but none lays claim to it as of right, because none of them has any special rights over the others. A by-product of such a situation is that the interaction may be directed away from competition for control and toward the collaboration needed for the group jointly to carry out their task. The subject-matter, the way it is approached, the order of speaking, and the participants' relative influence upon these are all decided during the interaction, not claimed and conceded as part of a prior role. One participant's view of what is going on is no more valid than another's. This interplay between alternative frames of reference constitutes the social reality which our account seeks to describe.

In order to deal with this multisemic character of dialogue we propose the theoretical construct which we call Frame. Every time a participant in dialogue makes an utterance he offers to the other participant two Frames, one referring to subject-matter which will be called Content Frame and the other referring to the interactive relationship and called Interaction Frame.

Briefly, by Content Frame we mean this: when Participant A speaks, his utterance, for him, carries with it a framework of implicit relevant knowledge, and this constitutes the Offered Content Frame. Participant B *understands* this utterance by attributing to it a framework of implicit relevant knowledge, and this constitutes an Attributed Content Frame. Participant C will understand the same utterance by similarly assigning to it a frame of reference, another Attributed Content Frame. Thus, in the example cited at the beginning of this section we saw the boys move from a roughly shared Content Frame referring to space suits into a Frame referring to diving suits. The importance of the shift of Frame is that it constitutes a shift in the realm of tacit knowledge needed for understanding. "It stops it from pushing it in" gains much of its referential meaning from the "diving suit" Frame.

An Interaction Frame is being offered in the very same utterance as is the Content Frame, since Participant A's utterance implies something about the interactive relationship they are taking part in. He may make a peremptory demand for a reply, or offer a hesitant opinion for comment. The Interaction Frame may (as in a typical lesson) imply that the speaker thinks he occupies a role which gives him a positional right to make such a demand; or it may be the expression of a personal and temporary bid for control. Thus, the Interaction Frame includes both the speaker's attempts to guide the course of the immediate interaction and his implicit long-term claims to personal and positional relationships. It is clear that the speaker's Frames may have more or less relationship to the hearer's Frames, according to such matters as their degree of common knowledge, intimacy, and so on. Appendix B gives a description of a few minutes of group discussion in which the negotiation of Interaction Frame and Content Frame are separately annotated.

The use of the concept of Frame frees us from any need to assign a determinate and unchanging meaning either to the content of an utterance or to its significance as a move in the interaction. It aids the observer to deal with: the different interpretations held by different participants; the ebb and flow during a conversation between more sharply defined Frames and those moments when Frames are blurred because in flux or mutually contradictory; and the dual aspect of the necessary tacit knowledge, which refers in one direction toward supplying a context for the subject matter and in the other toward sets of expectations about the social meaning of actions. To sum up, Frames refer to participants' implicit expectations about (a) what they are talking about, and (b) their relationship and communicative behavior. Frames are offered by those who speak and interpreted by those who listen. They change constantly in the course of a conversation—a fluidity and instability which in the potential for soft focus, for dissolution of what seemed clear, for movement, and for multiplicity of choice of perspective is close metaphorically to the cinematic notion of frame—and not all to the idea of boundary that is carried by the metaphor of a picture frame.

Joint Inquiry

We turn now to the role of questions and answers in the collaboration through which these students constructed shared meanings. Since each student brings a different set of frames to the problem issue, each approaches it from a unique perspective. If the members of a group are to advance their understanding through talk, these

differences of perspective must be interrelated and their discontinuities used to generate new and more inclusive understanding. As
the extracts discussed in Chapters 2 and 3 showed, groups differed
in the extent to which they supported an individual member's attempts to relate other participants' viewpoints to his own and to use
the other's viewpoint in problem solving.

Such negotiation between differing viewpoints plays an important
part in the development of new meanings in group discussion.
Awareness of the validity of a divergent perspective is one of the ways
through which one can come to see one's own perspective not as absolute but as hypothetical and therefore open to modification: producing internal change through seeing one's own views from the vantage
point of the other. The different view needs to be voiced, but it also
needs to be voiced in a way that means we will not reject this point of
difference out of hand but will engage and negotiate with it. In communicative terms, this engagement depends upon the use of those devices whereby members of the group ask for one another's opinions, encourage explicitness, pinpoint differences, and inter-relate viewpoints.
Initially it seemed to us that questions would be a prime means of per-
forming all of these, and we turned our attention to them.

We began by looking at the relationship between question forms
and questioning functions. We used a set of criteria that drew on
linguistic analysis to classify utterances or parts of utterances as
questions or statements. These criteria included the use of interrogative words (such as *why, when, how*), intonation, word order, and
the use of the word *do* (as in "do you live here?"). Another important question form which we distinguished in our materials was the
use of tag questions (as in "you live here, don't you?"). For a while
we tried approaching the questions in our data via Harrah's (1963)
paradoxical idea that questions are really statements. And we
looked at the kinds of replies that different question forms (for instance open questions) might elicit, as well as at the cognitive bur-
den which different question forms might place on either question
poser or question answerer. We went through quite a lengthy exercise of identifying and then classifying individual questions from
our data, using these different approaches.

However, despite the effort we put into this we did not find it
helpful. As with earlier phases of our analysis, we found we could
not make sense of the purposes to which questions were being put
if we looked at isolated cases out of context. We had to look back at
what had gone before and forward to what followed.

Take, for example, this question asked earlier in a discussion of
Steinbeck's novel *The Pearl* (the students had read only the early
part of the book):

What do you think that'll happen later on in the book, when we've
read it, you know, what will happen to the pearl, and to the doctor and everything? Will it all turn out happily, and that, or will,
you know, somebody die or something like that? (Marianne in
Group 1 talking about *The Pearl*).

This question proposes strict limits for the range of relevant replies:
the other students are first invited to make predictions, then these
predictions are given some specific reference to "the pearl, and the
doctor and everything," and then the range of appropriate replies is
narrowed still further towards happy endings or (as a contrast apparently) someone's death. Thus, the question sets up a Content
Frame which implicitly constrains what follows in the conversation. (This, by the way, appears to be what Harrah [1963] meant
when he treated questions as statements.) The other members of the
group may ignore the Frame presented in the question, they may
adopt and develop it, or they may adapt and change it. If they adopt
or adapt the Frame it becomes part of the implicit shared knowledge
which will underlie the remainder of their discussion of the topic.

At first sight, one clear and specific message in question forms
is to indicate the handing over of the speech role to another speaker.
However, questioning is also a social act and it carries an
Interaction Frame as well. Relationships are developed, maintained,
and changed through questions and answers alongside the exchange
of information or the construction of knowledge. Questions—like
answers and statements—carry messages about the social relations
that are ongoing in the conversation. It is clear from our analysis of
Frames, above, that equally explicit statements about speech roles,
laying claim to the speech role, deputing it to someone else—attempts at dominance—can be made alike by questions or statements. What then becomes important from the standpoint of sustaining dialogue is the extent to which either questions or statements indicate acceptance (or rejection) of the validity of other
viewpoints and the strength with which they lay claim to the right
to speak by virtue of position. We noted in Chapter 3 that the use of
chairperson-like moves—teacher's moves used by participants—
often brought exploration of a topic to a halt. (In this category we
would include rhetorical questions used for purposes of social control.) To illustrate this process in action we turn to another example
from our data.

In the example below, Group 3 members are discussing the
planning problems of National Parks, considering especially how to
reconcile the needs of varied uses such as tourism, farming, indus-
try, outdoor pursuits, and so on. The task card mentions suggestions

which have been made for the provision in the Lake District of cinemas, caravan sites, restaurants and so on. They have all agreed that
cinemas and night clubs should not be built in the Lakes, when
Margaret suddenly spots something on the task card which she
wishes to query:

37. Margaret: Any how if they've got a caravan site, what do they want a camping site and all for? And if they've got a restaurant what do they want a refreshment stall for? (Laughter)
Well it's true, what do they want them all for?

At first sight, here are three Wh questions; formal analysis would classify these as open questions. Margaret is asking the group what justification there might be for the provision of these facilities. Or is she? She is speaking in an angry tone of voice, and she prefaces the questions with signs that maybe she is not requesting another point of view. Is she asking the group a question, or is she daring them to disagree with her?

38. Robert: Well a restaurant's really for people who want to have a meal, and, a, and, a refreshment stall is for people who want a snack like a hot dog or a drink.

Robert takes a chance on the first interpretation. In modest tones, he shows how restaurants and refreshment stalls serve different needs, and supplies a justification for the provision of both of them.

39. Christine: Well they can go away

Christine strongly rejects Robert's contribution.

40. Margaret: What do they want a kiosk for, just to drink, ugh, it's stupid. What do they want a kiosk for?

Margaret indicates that she sees Robert's reply at 38 not as compliance with her request for reason, but as disagreement with a view she holds strongly—that these facilities are unnecessary. She rejects this alternative viewpoint most strongly.

41. Robert: Anyway, I don't think there ought to be tennis courts.

Robert has learned his lesson. He is not deceived by the question format of Margaret's 40 again. His attempt at 38 to supply reasons he thought were being requested has earned him verbal punishment. Now he changes the subject, implicitly accepting the force of Margaret's Interaction Frame.

We now return to a group whose members on this occasion ask each other hardly any questions, but who nevertheless hand over speech roles to each other in collaborative fashion. Group 1 has read the transcript of an interview with a young delinquent, and they have been asked to discuss *The Causes of Vandalism*.

3. David: I think the area you live in, er, could affect the way they behave because when there's other gangs around you, I think it, er, you know, makes you want to fight too if you see them all, fighting and that, it looks like fun and so he'll just join in

David states that he thinks that peer group influence is a factor in gang violence. There are several markers which indicate that this is a tentatively held view: "I think," "er," "I think it, er." This is not a dogmatic statement with which other participants will disagree at their peril, but an attempt to get the ball rolling. This is a contribution which can be built on and extended, as Jonathan does at 4.

4. Jonathan: Yes, he only, only, he'll only start fighting if other people do

The "Yes" acknowledges David's line of thought before extending it.

5. Marianne: And he thinks that the only way he can make himself, big, and make himself a somebody, is to prove to people that he is, big and is, tough and fight, and can fight all the time

Marianne connects her utterance to those preceding with the "and" and also by further extension of the ongoing line of thought.

A little later the same group continues:

15. Marianne: They seem to have their own cafés that they think their own, they own, and nobody else can come in . . . but I, I think all this is partly because of his upbringing, and the way he was treat when his, tre-treated when he was little.

16. David: Well I think vandalism is, how it comes about is, they should, should have, erm, more facilities for people messing about.

17. Jonathan: Yes, but they just reject these facilities because they'll think they're no good, and that.

18. David: Yes. Well I don't, I don't mean like—just like wrecking them. Don't mean like youth clubs, more, erm, discotheques and that, where, where over fifteen

19. Jonathan: Yes, but all they do is fight there.

20. Marianne: The, they can only go round in big gangs. They don't think of . . .

21. David: Well, none of them'll fight by their selves.

Through this extract, we hear the exchange of viewpoints about what the causes of vandalism might be. None of them is stated dogmatically, and no one person either lays explicit claim to the role of speaker or nominates anyone else to speak. Utterances follow each other smoothly. After pauses have indicated that one person has temporarily come to the end of what he has to say, another group member gives voice to his own thoughts. Note how tightly connected the content of the exchange is. These students are exploring collectively what they know. Where someone disagrees with the content of a previous utterance as at 17, they make a gentle qualification, not a full-blown disagreement. None of these students is trying either to manage the talk, or to get someone else to take responsibility for it: rather, they share, collaboratively, in the joint construction of an understanding. Speech roles are left fluid, such that it is open to any participant to contribute when he likes, rather than being either nominated to do so or stopped from doing so by other members. The whole exchange is carried out by statements. Yet these statements are a very effective way of eliciting another person's viewpoint.

Thus, although a question or statement form considered alone may function—all else being equal—as an interrogative or assertive move, in conversation this information is frequently overruled by interpretations drawn from the larger context, many of them unspoken. An overemphasis on forms results from a specific method of analysis, namely the consideration of isolated utterances only. Our examination of situated continuous discourse led us to believe that question and non-question forms may be used to make similar claims about speech roles, that is, to offer similar Interaction Frames.

Some studies have placed a heavy emphasis on *why* questions, believing them to be cognitively more useful than yes-no questions, seeing the former as *open* and the latter as *closed*, that is, as able to be answered by simple *yes* or *no* answers. In our data we found the relationship to be rather more complex than this. *Why* and other *wh* questions are not necessarily open-ended in terms of the answer they require. They may be constructed not from gaps in a conceptual framework but from the lack of a conceptual framework at all. Similarly, yes-no questions did not necessarily close down allowable replies to simple affirmation or negation. They often seemed to us to be evidence of successful cognitive functioning, in that the framing of a yes-no question may require more information and structuring on the part of a questioner than is requested by a *wh* question.

We can illustrate this latter point by reference to data from the study of small groups of primary school students engaged in computer-based learning, already discussed in Chapter 5 (Fisher 1993a). These researchers noted that in sessions on educational games software the computer:

> is generally the participant taking all the "complicated" decisions, transforming the students' minimal input (generally a single key press) into attractive, dynamic and complex representations which are of a completely different nature from the original input." (106)

In such a context the student's choice of response is constrained within the binary logic which structures the software. The complexity of the apparently "new" structures which are called up derives from the adult writer of the computer software who has framed what are in effect a series of *yes-no* questions, using knowledge and understanding at a far higher level than that as yet available to the students.

The structures offered by the computer software in that example could not be re-shaped by the students. Their options were limited to influencing the route taken through them via replies to pre-fixed choices. The context for our groups was rather different, and there are several examples in our data in which the collaborative extension and collaboration of a yes-no question by another member of the group seemed to arise from the framework of joint inquiry which the students shared, that is, from the Interaction Frame. Both these processes are shown at work in the next example which comes from a group talking about a science task concerned with work and energy.

David: Is there, is there any, any energy used when you let a wheel go down a hill?

Barbara: Yes.

Marianne: Yes, because you need, energy to push it off, don't you?

Bill: Yes.

David: Well, you're not, you're not pushing it off, are you, you're just letting it go?

In this case the yes-no form of question considered as a sentence could formally be said to require the respondent to commit himself only to "Yes" or "No." However, its context in problem-solving discussion makes it function also as a demand for fellow participants to go on beyond the terms offered by the question and to construct supporting propositions. We might ask ourselves how we would have understood the exchange if it had ended after Barbara's reply of "Yes." This would have seemed like a rejection of the whole of David's lead. In such a discussion as this the extension of an answer

beyond yes or no may operate as an indication of willingness to collaborate in a particular strategy; and a question may be posed in this
form among those particular participants with the confidence that
the social, as well as the cognitive, message will be understood.

To summarize the role we see for questions and answers we see
both questions and statements as a means to create new structures
and understandings. We do not believe there is any necessary coor-
dination between the form in which a question is posed and its cognitive power. What the members of our group gained in understanding from the exchange of questions and answers related not to
the form of the question but to the interpretation placed upon them.
This depended, quite crucially, on the social relationships within
the group. Much of the collaboration that permits the creation of
new understanding goes on by invitations to other groups to contribute—sometimes (but not always) posed in the form of questions.
In the example quoted above, to reply merely with "yes" or "no"
would be to opt out of the social relationships set up in the groups.
This would amount to redefining the situation from one where all
group members jointly shaped their own learning to one where one
particular group member reserved the right to monitor and structure
the learning process—as, for example, a teacher might. Refusing the
invitation to construct would not only take the development of cognitive understandings no further at that given point; it would also
undermine the social basis of joint collaboration.

In practice, therefore, we found that inquiry might progress
in utterances posed in any form. Either questions or statements
that offered appropriate Interaction Frames could act as tentative
attempts to arrive at a shared framework. Not only *tag* questions,
but statements and jointly-constructed utterances acted to ensure that the contributions made by other voices in the group
could be incorporated into the joint framework of meaning as it
developed.

David's question about whether energy is used when a wheel is
allowed to roll down a hill takes the listener for a person who "actively answers and reacts" rather than one who "passively understands." The quoted words are those of Bakhtin (1981, 280) who is
discussing at this point the difference between a word or a sentence
studied as an example for linguistic analysis and a word or a sentence spoken in live conversation. Bakhtin makes the point that any
word spoken in dialogic interaction is shaped with the pre-suppo-
sition of a reply already within it. The speaker orients what he says
"toward the specific conceptual horizon, toward the specific word
of the listener" (Bakhtin 1981, 282). It is shaped by what the speaker
knows, guesses, or believes about the "subjective belief system of

the listener" (282). This means that the other is already present in the speaker's utterance. The speaker's anticipation of this response is seen by Bakhtin as crucial to the development of understanding: "Understanding comes to fruition only in the response" (282). We should like to link this idea of "responsive understanding" (Bakhtin, 280) to another mechanism of joint inquiry, the use of hypothetical cases.

We demonstrated in Chapter 3 the importance of hypothetical cases which were used, implicitly, as a form of generalization and therefore as a means of testing the range and applicability of a developing view. Vygotsky (1992), drawing on Sapir (1971) considered that generalization is essential to the development of meaning. We cannot describe our own thoughts or experiences to somebody else without referring our listener to "some known class or group of phenomena" (6). He goes on:

> Such reference, however, already requires generalization. Therefore, communication presupposes generalization and development of word meaning; generalization, thus, becomes possible in the course of communication. The higher, specifically human forms of psychological communication are possible because man's reflection of reality is carried out in generalized concepts. [. . . .] real understanding and communication will be achieved only through generalization and conceptual designation of my experience. (7–8)

The hypotheticality of these viewpoints ("say he might be an old man, a friend like") serve, we suggested, the extremely important function of permitting the accord of validity to another's viewpoints—even if they clash with one's own. This provides more than social cohesion, in that encountering a viewpoint which is deemed to be both different and valid is what nudges the students towards finding a new formulation in which both are meaningful. In a group, the flashes of the insight which might come to an individual set the social task of finding a way of expressing it that does not compromise the collegial relationship of joint effort by a claim to prior knowledge.

The other side of this coin is that strategies adopted to find social solutions to the existence of these differences of opinion set the cognitive task of establishing overarching principles which inter-relate the two. The ascription of meaningfulness to each other's attempts to make sense of the world, the expression of different opinions in a way that qualifies or extends what has gone before, the close attentiveness to what others have said which can be seen both in acceptance and extension or in disagreement (expressed in a way that acknowledges the other as equal), and qualification (the use of supportive behaviors in speech, tone, and gesture), all these show the cognitive and the social going hand in hand.

We argued in Chapter 2 that the four key moves that form the staple of collaborative dialogue—initiating, eliciting, qualifying and extending—are not individual skills but are a function of group discussion. These moves, like the cognitive and interactional frames which form the micro-politics of small group discussions, are what permit the dialogic articulation and inter-relation of different points of view. Vygotsky argued that the only good learning is learning ahead of development. We would add to this, with Voloshinov, that "any true understanding is dialogic in nature" (Voloshinov 1975, 102).

To conclude this chapter, we now want to review our discussion so far in the context of Bakhtin's concept of dialogue.

Dialogue and the Generation of New Meaning

The word *dialogue* is often used interchangeably with words such as *conversation* or *discussion*. In the analysis of our groups' communication which we have summarized in this book we have drawn attention to certain features of the way members talk and develop understanding together. In this section we shall argue that the presence of these features makes at least some parts of the discussions of some of our groups different in certain important ways from the ordinary run of conversations or discussions. We used the term *dialogue* in the first version of our book when discussing these features—initially more in line with the dictionary definition which conveys "a conversation between two or more persons" (Shorter Oxford English Dictionary). However, in developing the concepts of Content and Interaction Frames and in noting that they could be offered (or attributed) in stronger or weaker forms according to the roles which participants assume in different educational contexts, we began to use the word dialogue in a way that set it out from other potential modes of interaction.

Since then, the word *dialogue* has come to be used in the psychology of education (Wertsch 1985, 1991), social theory (Göranzon and Florin 1992, Holquist 1990, Shotter 1993a and 1993b) and cultural analysis (Gardiner 1992, Hirschkop and Shepherd 1989)) in a special way which is based on the work of Bakhtin (1981). We want to highlight some of the features of talk in these groups with Bakhtin's ideas on dialogue in mind. The features to which we shall be drawing attention here are: difference of perspective, mutual attention, the use of hypothetical cases, tentativeness, the absence of prior roles by right, mutual support, and lack of closure. As we revisit these features we shall draw out connections with Bakhtin's idea of dialogue. Then, in the last section of this chapter, we will use this dialogic approach to sharpen the point that the use of small discussion groups should not be viewed as a technique, but as an approach to learning and development which brings—and needs— new relationships between the knower and what is known. First, however, we should like to preface this discussion with a brief summary of some aspects of Bakhtin's thinking.

Bakhtin and Dialogism

The concept of dialogue is obviously not new: a long philosophical tradition shows otherwise. Bakhtin's work, however, has brought the theoretical framework provided by the idea of dialogue to bear upon the development of the modern world, examining the characteristics of the forms of art that have been created to represent and explore that world and in particular the novel, which Bakhtin sees quintessentially as a means by which an author captures and conveys the multiplicity of voices that speak around him.

Bakhtin's concept of dialogue is predicated on a view of all discourse as situated in and mediated by context. This underlying relativism is based on the observation that speakers occupy a unique and unreplaceable position in relation to others. The words of a speaker carry assumptions and implications tied to the moment and the position from which they are spoken. These assumptions and implications in turn create a new context for the words of the next speaker. A word is spoken into this context, directed towards fleeting and momentary impressions of the responsive answer of the listener—so that a word never belongs to a speaker alone, but always is influenced by the intentions of others. To participate in a dialogue is to act as a speaking voice, and this can be achieved not only face to face in living dialogue but also, for instance, by expressing the assimilation of and struggle with the words of others in a work of prose art. A prose text, therefore, can be thought of always as having multiple authorship. Although Bakhtin sees dialogue as intrinsic to the human condition, he notes the development of different modes of discourse which may tend more towards monologue or to dialogue. He makes a distinction between authoritative discourse— the discourse of courts, of professional powers, of instruction— which comes as a given, fused with the authority to which it gives expression, and internally persuasive discourse which can be freely developed by speakers and applied to new material. This development and application is not easy; Bakhtin thinks of it as a struggle with other alien viewpoints, but it is a struggle which leads to "even newer ways to mean" (Bakhtin 1981, 346).

With this by way of introduction we now continue our review of our discussion so far with Bakhtin's concept of dialogue in mind.

Difference of Perspective

The expectation that small group discussions would afford the opportunity to encounter different viewpoints was, of course, the starting point for our research, and we have shown how the students brought different perspectives to the tasks at hand. The differences in their views varied in different groups and at different points in their tasks.

Bakhtin's notion of dialogue is based on this notion of difference and of encounters between difference. Nor is this an abstract notion; it is a practical and concrete one. Difference of perspective derives not only from the uniqueness of experience from which each of us speaks. It has a concrete base in our physical stance to the world as Michael Holquist elucidates in his commentary on Bakhtin (Holquist 1990, 165). (You can see the back of my head; I can see yours; when you look at me you can see the background from which I speak and vice versa.) At every second in a conversation speakers occupy different positions, a difference that is also made up of the different previous knowledge that they each bring to the encounter, based on their different past experiences. Bakhtin characterises these differences as "two consciousnesses, two language-intentions, two *voices*" (360). We are used to talking about difference in a way that assumes we must choose between them, that one of them must have priority, or that one must win out over the other. This is the dialectical view of the world that is enshrined in the formal logic of western philosophy.

Bakhtin's concept of dialogue gives us something quite different because it suggests the possibility of what Clark and Holquist (1984) have called "not a dialectical either/or, but a dialogic both/and" (7). The concept of dialogue suggests that rather than choosing between them, elements from one participant's perspective will influence and become part of what the other says when it is next his turn to speak, and that the same will happen in return. From a dialogic standpoint, the word spoken is never wholly the speaker's own—it always has within it elements of other people's ideas and intentions. We never speak into a void—there is always a history of what other people have said or done, and we respond to these even as we speak. In responding to others, we are influenced by their difference. The means for expressing this difference in a way that is responsive to the other is through speaking, through using one's voice—and also through listening to what the other has to say.

In Chapters 2 and 3 and in this chapter, we have traced the ways in which differences of viewpoint were articulated and used in the groups. We also showed examples where, from time to time, groups simply accepted a different viewpoint as uttered and did not work on it or engage with it. These were occasions where groups failed to develop their understanding further; in accepting what one voice said without examining it in the light of the knowledge that could have been expressed by other voices, what had just been said became dead from the point of view of new insight. From a Bakhtinian standpoint one would say that although, formally, these exchanges look like a conversation and can be set out like the dialogue in a play, the students' discourse had become, at these points, to some degree monologized (Bakhtin 1986, 163). It is difference of perspective that provides the inner life of new understanding.

Mutual Attention

Another feature of these discussions we highlighted was the careful attention paid by the students to each other's utterances. In this way the replies through which the attention was paid, often through qualifying and extending moves, took on particular importance. The students determined the context which made it possible for a next probing step to be taken, the next offering to be put forward for joint examination. We described how this mutual attention is manifested in replies which took on board and responded to (even if disagreeing with) what had just been said, as a socially and cognitively combined act that transcended surface linguistic forms such as question/answer.

This finds correspondence in Bakhtin's conceptualization of each spoken word being "oriented to an answer" (Bakhtin 1981, 280) leading him to suggest that it is the rejoinder or the response that has primacy on the development of understanding (1981, 282). The rejoinder from another person will contain something alien in it, but if it is *responsive* in a way that reciprocates the speaker's care in orienting what he says to what he knows of the speaker's thought-world at that time, then the respondent (simultaneously a speaker) and the speaker (simultaneously a respondent) create a new "combined context" (1981, 284) for the next utterance in the sequence. Dialogue accordingly, pays attention to the other. For this reason classrooms founded on dialogic discourse may avoid or diminish displays of asocial or antisocial attention-seeking behavior. In dia-

logue the participant "counts on" such an understanding and because of that orients his own utterance "toward the specific world
of the listener" (1981, 282). Each participant in a dialogue not only
answers responsively but is answerable; this is the moral dimension
to participation in dialogue: "the individual must become answerable through and through" (Bakhtin 1990, 2).

Hypothetical Cases

We discussed in some detail the strategy of setting up hypothetical
cases that the students used. Bakhtin suggests that the process of
understanding is achieved by liberating oneself from ideas that have
seemed authoritative so far; he speaks of this as a process of struggle. Something that one used to take for granted is now something
one has begun to resist.

Such a struggle is aided by experimentally putting into words—
almost as if from another speaker—a potentially persuasive idea
which

> is questioned, [. . .] is put in a new situation in order to expose its
> weak sides, to get a feel for its boundaries [. . . .] (Bakhtin 1981,
> 348).

Putting hypothetical viewpoints into words in this way permits one
"to guess, to imagine." Such experimental guesswork" (1981, 347)
is dialogic because it accords a voice to another point of view, even
though there may not be a different speaker physically present to
express it. It is as if it is attributed to another voice. This process of
"creatively erecting potential discourses" (1981, 353) which our students called on is a dialogic way of coming to know, a way of developing fresh understandings by opening up new potential features
of a situation to examination.

Tentativeness and Absence of Prior Roles by Right

One pronounced characteristic of the way our students worked together was, in successful groups, the tentativeness with which they
proffered views. We described how a view tentatively put forward
might be worked with for a little while, then perhaps dropped, only
to be returned to and reworked on successive occasions in a cyclical
process until a formulation emerged that all the students in the
group were happy with. That formulation would then serve as the
starting point for further exploration of another issue. It was this tentativeness that permitted other group members to take up and work
on viewpoints. Tentativeness made clear that an idea put forward

was a contribution to a common endeavour, that the speaker put the idea forward as something that could be examined, elaborated, interrogated, qualified, or have limits set to it by others. We have used the term *put forward* above and would like to emphasize here the contribution to going *forward*—to the movement into the new which this tentativeness achieved. We linked it to the roles which the students occupied in relation to each other. None of them had prior roles by right which would give their formulation priority as a teacher's does. We noted that the use of *chairperson's* moves was rare and that where they did occur they often achieved premature closure because they ruptured the commonality of exploration in which the group's work was based. Such moves protect an utterance from the inquiry of others and so—temporarily at least—prevent the process of mutual interrogation which takes understanding forward.

One of the key means by which this tentativeness and the renunciation of claims to prior knowledge were achieved was through accenting the individual nature of an utterance while at the same time inviting another's view. This was often achieved through beginning with "I think" and ending with a tag question. Intonation and the incorporation into an utterance of part of a previous speaker's thought also played their part. In these ways, what was put forward was not something that had to be accepted as it was or swallowed whole by other participants but was something that already carried within it the grounds of its own challenge. Bakhtin's theory sees this proffering of "differing nuances of meaning" (1981, 270), this provision of a mix of voices in one utterance as one of the main features of dialogue. An utterance in dialogue is part of an "elastic environment of the other" (Bakhtin 1981, 276). The utterance "can not fail to brush up against thousands of living dialogic threads" (276) whereas the absolute offered as right-in-itself closes itself off to further inquiry and therefore to further illumination. We saw that in groups where a participant strongly put something forward as absolute, this was a point of closure. Bakhtin's characterization of the word in dialogue as the "word with a sideways glance" finds living manifestations in the tentativeness of these discussions.

Mutual Support

By contrast with the occasional dogmatic utterances which fractured the collaborative inquiry of the groups, the mutual support which participants gave to each other ("go on, go on") emphasized the importance attributed to another's point of view. Another's view was important because it was not one's own. It was valuable because it was different. The students needed to encounter and engage with these differences to progress their joint inquiry. Mutual support serves another purpose of reminding speakers who their listeners are and what they know—or don't know—already. It is a way of helping co-speakers attune themselves to each other, of bringing forth what they each have to say "in contact with one another" (Bakhtin 1981, 361).

We noted that one important mode of mutual support was the acceptance and qualification or extension of what someone else had just said. Sometimes this extended to the point of constructing a joint utterance, begun by one speaker, finished by another. Mutual support, in its various ways, meant that what one person said did not represent just that one person's private intentions. As students spoke they responded to the intentions of the other people who were sharing in the joint inquiry, the word they spoke even as they spoke was "directing its purposiveness outward" (1981, 354).

The internal logic of one utterance encountered and responded to the internal logic of another—so that mutual support created a process of mixing. Bakhtin (1981) refers to utterances that mix or mingle together in this way as *hybrids* which he sees as "profoundly productive [..] pregnant with potential for new world views" (1981, p. 360). As in the materials we quote he notes that these hybridized constructions do not necessarily fuse together into finished utterances. It is as if one utterance contains two elements that can talk to each other.

The creation of such hybrids presupposes not only two different viewpoints but the inter-relationship of these viewpoints if they are to create new meaning by mixing together. The expression of these differences, in our groups, was aided by the mutual support which in the first place acknowledged them as different, in the second place encouraged their expression, and in the third place helped participants attune their voicing of these different views to the state of readiness and responsiveness of their listeners. The new thoughts that became actual for the first time in the discussions became so in anticipation of the other's responses, which are made manifest in the "links in the chain of speech communication" (Bakhtin 1986, 94).

Lack of Closure

The final feature of the discussions to which we wish to draw attention is lack of closure. We demonstrated how the groups returned to an issue over and again, opening up some new aspect of it for discussion, rather than working through issues as a series of discrete agenda items which, once discussed, were complete and closed. This mode of working—which would have been the despair of a committee—created an openness to further inquiry, further examination, which was what took the groups forward into new conceptual territory.   This "eternal re-thinking and re-evaluating" (1981, 31) is part of what Bakhtin saw as intrinsic to the process of world-making that comes from focusing on the present rather than on the past. Our groups addressed the present of what each of them successively said and did, not the completed past of, for instance, a teacher's presentation. Addressing the present brings the future into play because it is intrinsic to the present that "the final word has not yet been spoken" (1981, 30).

One can make a link here with what we have said about tentativeness: the absence of a final word—inconclusiveness—is also what opens up the very possibility of a future. What is concluded has no present and therefore no future, only a past. Equally, what is complete cannot adjust itself to, or respond to, another speaker—"what is complete is hopelessly ready made" (1981, 34). For that reason it is ill-suited to the process of creating new meaning.

Incompleteness means that we can take a word into new contexts (in our groups, these new contexts were created by successive phases of discussion)

> attach it to new material, put it in a new situation in order to wrest new answers from it. (346)

and so create new meanings from it. Bakhtin sees this incompleteness as arising from the fact that what is said must always respond to something—somewhere—that has already been said. We speak to what we know about what other people know, from our contact with them, but this raises the possibility of what is unknown, that will form a new context. Proximity, contact, knowledge of the other, and dialogic interaction with the other create the zone of possible development—which is, after all, possible but not necessary. Inconclusiveness, therefore, is intrinsic to development.

Reflecting on Frames

We described as *frames* the mechanisms we identified for interchanges of situated cognitive and social knowledge. From a Bakhtinian perspective one might think of frames as the manifestation in live discourse of what he called zones of contact. These zones always have claims upon them from somebody's voice, in dialogue claims from more than one voice. Framing is a way of framing another's speech as well as one's own, a way of bringing another's speech into contact with one's own, a way to "create a perspective" (1981, 358) for the speech of another, even to "penetrate into the interior of another's speech" (1981, 358). It is a way of "coming to know one's own belief system in someone else's system" (1981, 365).

Thus frames, as we found them in our materials are the places in a "zone of contact" or in a "zone of proximal development" in which two different viewpoints can *struggle* together. Frames are more than locations; they are *devices* for this struggle, a struggle which has the effect of bringing the live force of one viewpoint into the live force of another.

Dialogue, Knowing, and Education

We commented in our first chapter on the fact that our research design meant that in the two phases of our research we created two rather different contexts for the group discussions in the two phases of our research. In following a quasi-experimental model in our second phase we, all unwittingly, created contexts which breached many of the conditions for dialogue. The students in the second phase knew each other less well or perhaps not at all, were not used to working together in small groups, met together in this particular grouping only on this one occasion, did not have the chance to get to know us as researchers or to play back and discuss their work with us. It is not surprising that in this one-off, unfamiliar, not fully understood, brief occasion, students in this second phase were less likely to generate the exploratory, inquiring talk of students in the first phase of the research. Students in the first phase had the time and opportunity to develop their own learning purposes in the regularly-meeting groups. Students in the second phase could not develop their own purposes, by and large, except for a small number of students who already knew each other. It is not surprising that the breaches, the tensions, the problems, came primarily in this second phase of work—in which, with hindsight, we would say that we treated the students as objects of our research rather than as co-subjects.

It is easy to replicate in teaching the mistakes we made as researchers by treating small groups as a condition that can be applied to classrooms, as if they are a technique for doing familiar things differently. A technique is something applied from the outside for technical purposes on the assumption that the units to which it is applied may perform better (within given parameters) under this condition. However, as we have described small group work within this dialogic framework, it is a means for changing educational parameters and for changing the students who participate in it.

We said in Chapter 1 that we do not see small group discussion as a "cure-all" or as a substitute for other modes of classroom teaching. Some of the educational tasks that schools set out to do may well be better achieved by, for instance, teacher-led full class discussion, or presentations from the teacher, or private study by students or by practical sessions. Similarly, one would not expect group work to be of particular help if what is required is that students commit to memory existing pieces of information without changing them. This is the learning of what Vygotsky referred to as "past history" and of the kind of authoritative statements which Bakhtin described as "compact and inert." It is relatively easy to set up small groups in which students take turns at speaking but in which the truly dialogic aspects are minimal. This occurs when the way in which groups are set up and the tasks they are given to work on are designed, for whatever reason, in such a way as to preempt or prevent the dialogic features which we have set out above.

Vygotsky argued (1978, 89) that the only good learning was learning ahead of development. Bakhtin characterized all true learning as possessing a "stage of genius" (1981, 352). We see a resonance between these two, such that the idea of the stage of genius helps to explain the apparent paradox of Vygotsky's formulation. If we uncouple "learning" from the idea of its service to the past we can then design learning so as to generate the learner's future development. This does not yet exist; it has to be made. We hope we have shown that the materials of its making are social, through the dialogic interchange between peers of different points of view. If such are a teacher's purposes, then small group discussions, carefully-designed, can be a powerful means to support this development.

We should like to conclude with the final comments of our 1977 publication, where we considered the different forms of participation available to students in teacher-led settings and in the more collective relationships that we observed in our small group discussions. In these, we observed, group members were free to shift the topic, to try out new formulations and to explore alternatives, since none of the questions asked concealed positional claims to impose a frame on the discussion—to guide its direction or to judge the relevance of answers. The members of our groups cast their bread upon the waters. They were each others' resources, and most of their utterances were contributions to thinking. Their occasional questions did not seek to control but to invite; this is why they did not fall into easily recognizable functional categories, as do many of a teacher's utterances. Their questions were at the respondents' disposal, to utilize as they would.

It has become clear to us in the course of this study that the allocation of power affects how people take part in the formulating of knowledge. The effect of placing control of relevance in the hands of one person is to emphasize his content frame, and this will affect profoundly the basis upon which others participate. If on the other hand, alternative frames are open to negotiation, this will influence not only who takes part but also the knowledge which is celebrated. Thus, what is learned by discussion in a group of peers will be different in kind as well as content from what is learned from teachers. When the criteria of relevance are negotiated and not imposed, the Content Frames which participants develop in the course of negotiation are likely to bear more directly upon the learner's actions since they will be idiomatically related to the frames through which he is currently interpreting the world about him. As we pointed out earlier in this chapter, the very indeterminacy of the frames negotiated in our groups was a condition of their developing alternative meanings rather than rehearsing an established Content Frame taken over from a teacher.

It would be easy for an unsympathetic reader to dismiss such learning contemptuously as likely to be vague, unself-critical, or downright wrong. Although we were often impressed by the quality of the students' discussion, it is true that at times its quality was less satisfactory. Equally, not all the lessons carefully structured by teachers result in well-shaped or accurate learning. We must beware of contrasting small group talk with an idealized version of class-teaching. But we are not claiming that all educational purposes can be carried out in small groups; that would be absurd. Our study has made it clear that younger adolescents can under helpful circumstances carry out collaborative learning in small groups, and that at times they display impressive cognitive and social abilities. Our point is that to place responsibility in students' hands changes the nature of their learning by requiring them to negotiate their own criteria of relevance and truth. If schooling is to develop in young people the qualities needed for responsible adult life, such learning has an important place in the repertoire of the social relationships teachers have at their disposal.

Appendix A

The Tasks

The Pearl

In the introduction to *The Pearl*, John Steinbeck says that the story may be a parable and that, "perhaps everyone takes his own meaning from it."

Discuss among yourselves what you have found in the story so far—the "good and bad things, and black and white things and good and evil things" as Steinbeck says; and any points about the characters, the settings, the way the book is written, that you feel worth discussing.

Problems of National Parks

National parks provide:

- Mountains, lakes, open country, waterfalls, and farming land.
- National parks accommodate climbing, skiing, fell walking, camping, sailing, and swimming.
- People are demanding roads, camping sites, caravan [trailer] sites, hotels, car parks [parking lots], restaurants, refreshment stalls, kiosks, toilets, swimming pools, petrol stations, garages, tennis courts, cinemas, night clubs, and casinos.

How can these demands be met without spoiling the natural beauty and attractions?

Causes of Vandalism

An interview with Ron

A. "Yes, from then on I went with the Boys. I'd play dice and billiards with them, play the juke boxes, picking up jobs. That went on till the middle of last year, when I thought all this was getting me nowhere."

"The Boys? Well, our clique we could be about 100, 150. Once we went over to the East End, there were 200 of us in cars and lorries and vans; we went to fight against the Greeks and the Turkish down in the Commercial Road. There was a terrific punch-up. Only a few people got pulled in."

"Ordinary way, of course, there weren't so many. Our clique we'd meet in billiards halls, we'd play dice. For instance we might go to the Greek Caff and play the jukebox, me and a few mates, and one of us might say, 'Let's go over to Camberwell and have a punch-up.' So we'd go to a caff down that way, and one of us would say, 'Anyone here thinks he's a hard nut?' and then we'd bring out the Boys and there'd be a fight. Or else we'd try to get somebody out of a dance hall. We used to stand and look for a bit of bother, you know, someone'd look at us cheeky and we'd get him outside."

Q. "What about the fighting—how did you set about it?"

A. "Well, it'd start with fists like, and then somebody'd get rough. We used bottles and chains and hammers. . . . or we'd try to fight the [named group]. We used to shout at them in the street, 'You [deletion] bastards,' to try to stop them getting off buses, to frighten them. We'd often go for the [named group], we don't like them round here, we hate them."

Q. "Did you yourself like fighting?"

A. "Ever since I was a little kid I wanted to make people be frightened of me. . . . All along I had the ambition to be somebody. I never had the chance to be somebody. . . ."

(This interview was first published in T. R. Fyvel, *Insecure Offenders*, Chatto and Windus, 1961; the extract used here is taken from R.H. Poole and P.J. Shepherd (eds), *Impact*, Book 2, *Themes and Topics*, Heinemann, 1967.)

What do you think this interview tells you about the causes of vandalism?

Do you think that Ron's last comment is particularly relevant?

Work and Energy

We use the idea of *work* as a measure of how much *energy* changes from one form to another. *Work* is done when a force moves.

Here are some energy changes. Discuss them, and work out the ones in which work is done:

- Electricity to light in a light bulb
- Heat to movement in a steam engine
- Food to movement on a bicycle

Think of any other energy changes.
Is work always done when energy changes form?

Steve's Letter of Notice

Dear Sir,
You must think I'm crazy trying this one on me. Telling me it was a nice interesting job for the holidays. Just light work! I don't see YOU getting down on your knees on a concrete floor, not likely! AND they keep spitting and throwing down ice creams and fag ends all mixed together, it makes you sick. You must think I'm crazy.

Next time you want someone to do your dirty work you want to choose someone who's daft. I wouldn't be seen dead in the place. Not at that money. And that Sam in the kitchen with his jokes. You can keep it.

Yours faithfully,
Steve

Steve wrote this letter giving notice that he was leaving after spending the summer holidays working in the café. But after he'd written it, he remembered that summer jobs are hard to come by and that he might need a job there again next holidays. How do you think he should alter, or rewrite it, if he wants to be employed in the same café again?

Carbon Dioxide In Water

One person take the tube M. in your mouth and breathe in and out through your mouth until a change takes place in the lime water.

Q.   Why does the apparatus only let air in through one tube and only let air out through the other?"

LOOK AT THE ARRANGEMENT OF THE TUBES.

Q. Does the lime water change most in the in tube or the out tube?

Q. How is air that you breathe out different from air that you breathe in?

YOU WILL HAVE TO REMEMBER WHICH GAS IT IS THAT CAUSES THE CHANGE IN LIME WATER.

Figure Appendix A–1
Carbon Dioxide in Water

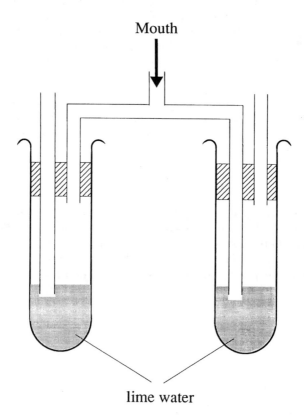

Mouth

lime water

Discussions Task

Sometimes discussions seem to work very well, and sometimes they don't seem to get off the ground. This happens in all discussions. We're trying to find out what helps make good discussions.

You're going to listen to a tape of yourselves talking about *The Pearl*. When you have listened to it, we'd like you to talk about it. We want to hear your ideas about what things help to make useful discussions.

Here are some questions that might help.

1. Which bits of the discussion went best? What kind of things seemed to help? What did people say that got the discussion moving?

2. When did the discussion come up against dead ends? Can you tell what caused this?

3. Have you learnt anything from hearing yourselves that will help you in tackling future discussions?

4. Do you think that discussing in a group is as useful as working on your own? Is it as useful as working in full class with the teacher?

Life in the Trenches

Discuss among yourselves life in the trenches during the First World War.

What was it like?

What sort of discomforts and dangers did the soldiers face?

What would you dislike most if you found yourself in a similar situation? The danger or the discomfort?

Bird's Eggs

1. Chip a small hole in the blunt end of the egg, and peep through it. What is there at this end of the egg? Why is it there?

2. Crack the egg into a dish, without breaking the yolk. Find a small white speck on the yolk. What do you think this is?

3. External fertilization is the method of reproduction used by frogs and fish. Do you think a bird's egg could be fertilized inside the hen's body? What makes you think so?

4. Will it be fertilized before the shell is put on, or after?

5. The mother hen turns her eggs occasionally? Why?

6. Look for coiled white strings in the egg white which attach the yolk to the shell. What are they there for?

Spaceman

We placed a corked bottle under a bell jar.

We pumped the air out of the bell jar with a vacuum pump.

Then the cork came out.

1. Discuss among yourselves the relationship between the pressure in the bottle and the pressure under the bell jar when all the air had been sucked out.

2. Why did the cork come out?

3. If a piece of rock hit a space ship and made a hole in it, what would happen to the air inside?

4. What would happen to the spaceman if he stepped out into space without a space suit on?

Causes of Gang Violence

Some teenage boys join gangs and spend a lot of their leisure time fighting other gangs.

They don't only fight in self-defense, but sometimes make an excuse to pick a fight.

They may start off by only fighting with their fists, but sometimes someone gets rough, and they start using bottles, chains, or knives.

Why do you think boys fight in gangs like this?

Appendix B

Interaction and Content Frames

Utterance number and pupil's name	Interaction frame	Content frame
19. Graham: "Number two, why did the cork come out?"	Claiming role of gatekeeper, Graham reads question from task card.	The Content Frame derives from the teacher who wrote the task card, which refers to an earlier lesson and to the frame then set up.
We've done that, haven't we?"	Gatekeeping and asking for approval of his gatekeeping move.	They assume a common frame and the content here switches momentarily to their conduct of the task.
20. Barry: "Yeah, we've done that.	Confirms Graham's move.	Conduct of task.
We've now done two, Tape.	Addresses tape recorder, making tacit assumptions that the recorder audience is not part of the group and does not share group meanings.	Conduct of task.
All right, if a piece of rock hit a spaceship and made a hole in, what would happen to the air?	Taking over the gatekeeping role, Barry signals a change of topic, and reads a new question (Question 3).	Although chosen by the teacher, this question has not been discussed before and so is open to interpretation.
All't air would come roo, rushing out wouldn't it? Er, all the air would come rushing out.	Answers question, asking for support, but excluding others from the floor.	Assumes sufficient consensus about the Content Frame implied in the question for a brief answer, without detailed explication, to be acceptable.
What would happen to the spaceman if he stepped out into space without a space suit on?"	Reads next question (No.4), still acting as gatekeeper.	This question from the teacher is also open to interpretation.
21. Alec: "Would suck everything out with it".	Challenges Barry's monopoly of the floor (both speaking at once).	Specifies as relevant to Question 3 details not mentioned by Barry, thus imposing a modification of the implicit Content Frame.
22. Barry: "Oh, he'd, he, all, all his, all his body would explode."	Trying to hold the floor.	Briefly indicates a Frame.
23. Graham: "He'd explode."	Competing for the floor.	Has now accepted move to Question 4. Frame so far common with Barry
24. Barry: "He'd expand, wouldn't he? He'd explode."	Competing for the floor.	Adds alternative construction to Frame.
25. Graham: "He'd just explode because erm, he's got pressure from inside the space ship inside him."	Competing for the floor	Explicates the Frame he is offering by beginning to analyse process.
26. Barry: "Yeah, yeah, he's not used to it really is he?"	Weakening his ploy with elements of acknowledgement and appeal.	Barry explicates part of his Frame.
27. Graham: "Well even so, even if he breathed out or something like that there's."	Graham has captured the floor.	Implicitly rejects part of Barry's frame on the basis of the previous utterance. Rejects possibility of adaptation to pressure, i.e. contradicting Barry's 'Not used to it'.
28. Barry: "Yeah."	Barry reduced to supporting role.	Preparing to accept Graham's Frame.
29. Graham: "Still't pressure that he's used to, inside him and there in't any pressure outside at all, so he gets, he just explodes."	Holds the floor.	Continues to expound own Frame in detail (without indicating whether its status is hypothetical.
30. Barry: "Yeah...How, does a pace, space suit stop it? Is there air inside?"	Asks for information, thus implicitly conceding expertise to Graham. (NB: Alec has remained silent ever since his original challenge at No.21 to Barry's control of the interaction).	Abandons own Frame and tries to grasp Graham's Frame.

174

Bibliography

Anderson, R.C. 1959. "Learning in Discussions." *Harvard Educational Review 29*:201–215

Baddeley, G., ed. 1992. *Learning Together Through Talk: Key Stages 1 & 2.* London: Hodder and Stoughton.

Baird, J., and I. Mitchell. 1986. *Improving the Quality of Teaching and Learning.* Melbourne: Monash University.

Bakhtin, M.M. 1981. *The Dialogic Imagination.* Austin: University of Texas Press.

———. 1986. *Speech Genres and other Late Essays.* Austin: University of Texas Press.

———. 1990. *Art and Answerability.* Austin: University of Texas Press.

Baldwin, J.A.M. 1976. *The Role of Small Group Discussion in the Acquisition of Geographical Concepts by Secondary School Pupils.* Unpublished M.A. thesis, University of Sheffield.

Barnes, D. 1976. 2d ed. 1992. *From Communication to Curriculum.* Portsmouth, N.H.: Boynton/Cook.

Barnes, D., and F. Todd. 1977. *Communication and Learning in Small Groups.* London: Routledge and Kegan Paul.

Bennett, N. et al. 1984. *The Quality of Pupil Learning Experiences.* Hillsdale, N.J.: Erlbaum.

Bennett, N., and A. Cass. 1989. "The Effects of Group Composition on Group Interactive Processes and Pupil Understanding." *British Educational Research Journal*, 15(1):19–32.

Bennett, N., and E. Dunne. 1992. *Managing Classroom Groups.* Hemel Hempstead: Simon and Schuster.

Bernstein, B. 1971. *On the Classification and Framing of Educational Knowledge.* In *Class, Codes and Control,* vol. 1. London: Routledge and Kegan Paul.

Biott, C. 1987. "Cooperative Group Work: Pupils' and Teachers' Membership and Participation." *Curriculum* 8(2).

Booth, D., and C. Thornley-Hall, eds. 1991a. *Classroom Talk.* Markham, Ont.: Pembroke.

———, eds. 1991b. *The Talk Curriculum.* Markham, Ont.: Pembroke.

Boydell, D. 1975. "Pupils' Behavior in Junior Classrooms." *British Journal of Educational Psychology* 45:122–9.

Brierley, Laura, Irena Casser, Pauline Loader, Kate Norman, Irene Shantry, Simon Wolfe, and Dave Wood. 1992. "No, We Ask You Questions." In Kate Norman, ed. *Thinking Voices. The Work of the National Oracy Project,* 215–223. London: Hodder and Stoughton.

Britton, J. Talking to Learn. In D. Barnes, J. Britton, and M. Torbe. 1969. 4th ed. 1991. *Language, the Learner and the School.* Portsmouth, N.H.: Boynton/Cook Heinemann.

Brown, Ann L., and A.S. Palincsar. 1989. Guided, Cooperative Learning and Individual Knowledge Acquisition. In L.B. Resnick, ed. *Knowing, Learning and Instruction: Essays in Honor of Robert Glaser.* 393–451. Hillsdale, N.J.: Erlbaum.

Brown, Ann L., Doris Ash, Martha Rutherford, Kathryn Nakagawa, Ann Gordon, and Joseph C. Campione. 1993. Distributed Expertise In The Classroom. In Gavriel Salomon, ed. *Distributed Cognitions. Psychological and Educational Considerations.* Cambridge: Cambridge University Press.

Brubaker, M., R. Payne, and K. Rickett, eds. 1990. *Perspectives on Small Group Learning.* Oakville, Ont.: Rubicon.

Carr, W., and S. Kemiss. 1986. *Becoming Critical: Knowing Through Action Research.* London: Falmer.

Clark, Katerina, and Michael Holquist. 1984. *Mikhail Bakhtin.* Cambridge: The Belknap Press of Harvard University Press.

Cohen et al. 1990. Treating Status Problems in the Cooperative Classroom. In Sharan 1990.

Corden, Roy. 1992. The Role of the Teacher. In Kate Norman, ed. *Thinking Voices. The Work of the National Oracy Project.* London: Hodder and Stoughton.

Day, R.R., ed. 1986. *Talking to Learn: Conversation in Second Language Acquisition.* Rowley, Mass.: Newbury House.

Delamont, S. 1983. *Interaction in the Classroom,* 2d ed. London: Methuen.

———. 1984. The Old Girl Network: Reflections on the Fieldwork at St. Luke's. In Robert G. Burgess, ed. *The Research Process In Educational Settings: Ten Case Studies.* London: The Falmer Press.

Denscombe, M. 1980. Pupil Strategies and the Open Classroom. In P. Woods, ed. *Pupil Strategies: Explorations in the Sociology of the School.* 50–73. London: Croom Helm.

Department of Education and Science. 1975. *Language for Life* (The Bullock Committee's Report). London: HMSO.

———. 1985. *Education for All: Report of a Committee of Inquiry into the Education of Children from Ethnic Minority Groups.* London: HMSO.

Des-Fountain, Jenny, and Alan Howe. 1992. Pupils Working Together on Understanding. In Kate Norman, ed. *Thinking Voices. The Work of the National Oracy Project.* 129–147. London: Hodder and Stoughton.

Dewhirst, W., and B. Wade. 1984. "Talking and Written Composition--the Primary Context." British Educational Research Journal 10(1):63–70.

Dix, Tonya. 1993. Cycles of Professional Growth: Evaluating Literature Discussion Groups. In Kathryn Mitchell Pierce and Carol J. Gilles, eds. Cycles of Meaning. 315–329. Portsmouth, N.H.: Heinemann.

Fisher, Eunice. 1993a. "Characteristics of Children's Talk at the Computer and Its Relationship to the Computer Software". Language and Education, vol. 7, no. 2:97–114.

———. 1993b. "Distinctive Features of Pupil-Pupil Classroom Talk and Their Relationship to Learning: How Discursive Exploration Might Be Encouraged". Language and Education: vol. 7, no. 4:239–257.

Florin, Magnus, Bo Göranzon, and Pehr Sällström. 1991. The Dialogue Seminar. In Bo Göranzon and Magnus Florin, eds. Dialogue and Technology: Art and Knowledge. London/New York: Springer-Verlag.

Galton, M., B. Simon, and P. Croll. 1980. Inside the Primary Classroom. London: Routledge and Kegan Paul.

Galton, M., and J. Williamson. 1992. Group Work in the Primary Classroom. London: Routledge.

Gardiner, Michael. 1992. The Dialogics of Critique. London: Routledge.

Gibson, J.J. 1979. The Ecological Approach to Visual Perception. Boston: Houghton Mifflin.

———. 1982. Reasons for Realism: Selected Essays of James J. Gibson. Hillsdale, N.J.: Erlbaum.

Harlen, W. 1985. Taking the Plunge. London: Heinemann.

Harrah, D. 1963. Communication: A Logical Model. Boston: Masschusetts Institutue of Technology Press.

Hirschkop, Ken, and David Shepherd. 1989. Bakhtin and Cultural Theory. Manchester: Manchester University Press.

Hoetker, J., and W.P. Ahlbrand. 1969. "The Persistence of the Recitation." American Educational Research Journal 6(2):145–167.

Holquist, Michael. 1990. Dialogism. Bakhtin and his World. London: Routledge.

Howe, A. 1988. Expanding Horizons: Teaching and Learning Through Whole Class Discussion. Sheffield: National Association for the Teaching of English.

Johnson, D., G. Maruyama, R. Johnson, D. Nelson, and L. Shaw. 1981. "Effects of Cooperative, Competitive and Individualistic Goal Structures in Achievement: A Meta Analysis." Psychological Bulletin 89:47–62.

Jones, P. 1988. Lip Service. Milton Keynes: Open University Press.

Kagan, S. 1985. Coop Coop: A Flexible Cooperative Learning Technique. In R. Slavin et al., eds. Learning to Cooperate, Cooperating to Learn. New York: Plenum Press.

Kemeny, H., ed. 1993. *Learning Together Through Talk: Key Stages 3 & 4.* London: Hodder and Stoughton.

Kemp, G. 1977. *The Turbulent Term of Tyke Tyler.* London: Faber.

Kozulin, Alex. 1986. "Vygotsky in Context." In Lev Vygotsky *Thought and Language.* Revised and edited by Alex Kozulin. xi–1vi. Cambridge: The Massachusetts Institute of Technology Press.

Lazarowitz, R., and G. Karsenty. 1990. Cooperative Learning and Students' Academic Achievement, Process Skills, Learning Environment, and Self-Esteem in Tenth Grade Biology Classrooms. In Sharan 1990.

Martin, N.C. et al. 1976. *Understanding Children Talking.* Harmondsworth: Penguin Books.

Mead, George H. 1934. *Mind, Self and Society.* Chicago: University of Chicago Press.

Moll, Luis C., and James B. Greenberg. 1990. Creating Zones of Possibilities: Combining Social Contexts for Instruction. In Luis C. Moll, ed. *Vygotsky and Education. Instructional Implications and Applications of Sociohistorical Psychology.* 319–348. Cambridge: Cambridge University Press.

Moll, Luis C., Javier Tapia, and Kathryn F. Whitmore. 1993. Living Knowledge: The Social Distribution of Cultural Resources for Thinking. In G. Salomon, ed. *Distributed Cognitions. Psychological and Educational Considerations.* Cambridge: Cambridge University Press.

Morrison, M., and P. Sandhu. 1993. Towards a Multilingual Pedagogy. In K. Norman, ed. 1993.

Nixon, J. 1981. *A Teacher's Guide to Action Research.* London: Grant McIntyre.

Norman, Kate, ed. 1992. *Thinking Voices. The Work of the National Oracy Project.* London: Hodder and Stoughton.

Pea, Roy D. 1993. Practices of Distributed Intelligence and Designs for Education. In G. Saloman, ed. *Distributed Cognitions. Psychological and Educational Considerations.* 47–87. Cambridge: Cambridge University Press.

Perret-Clermont, Anne-Nelly, Jean-Francois Perret, and Nancy Bell. 1991. The Social Construction of Meaning and Cognitive Activity in Elementary School Children. In Lauren B. Resnick et al., eds. *Perspectives on Socially Shared Cognition.* Washington, D.C.: American Psychological Association.

Phillips, T. 1985. Beyond Lip-Service: Discourse Development After the Age of Nine. In G. Wells, and J. Nicholls. *Language and Learning: An Interactional Perspective.* London and Philadelphia: Falmer Press.

Piaget, J. 1950. *The Psychology of Intelligence.* New York: Harcourt Brace.

———. 1960. *The Language and Thought of the Child.* London: Routledge and Kegal Paul. (First published 1928).

————. 1965. *The Moral Judgement of the Child.* New York: Free Press.

Pierce, K.M., C. Gilles, and D. Barnes, eds. 1993. *Cycles of Meaning.* Portsmouth, N.H.: Heinemann.

Preston, Dennis R. 1982. " 'Ritin Fowklower Daun' Rong: Folklorists' Failures in Phonology." *Journal of American Folklore* 95.377:304–26.

————. 1985. "The Li'l Abner Syndrome: Written Representations of Speech." *American Speech* 60.4:328–36.

Reid, J., P. Forrestal, and J. Cook. 1989. *Small Group Work in the Classroom.* Scarborough, W. Australia: Chalkface Press.

Resnick, Lauren B. 1991. Shared Cognition: Thinking as Social Practice. In L.B. Resnick et al., eds. *Perspectives on Socially Shared Cognition.* 1–20. Washington, D.C.: American Psychological Association.

Resnick, Lauren B., John M. Levine, and Stephanie D. Teasley. 1991. *Perspectives on Socially Shared Cognition.* Washington, D.C.: American Psychological Association.

Rogoff, Barbara. 1990. *Apprenticeship in Thinking: Cognitive Development in Social Context.* New York: Oxford University Press.

Ruddock, Jean. 1991. *Innovation and Change. Developing Involvement and Understanding.* Toronto, The Ontario Institute for Studies in Education: OISE Press.

Salman, Phillida, and Hilary Claire. 1984. *Classroom Collaboration.* London: Routledge and Kegan Paul.

Saloman, Gavriel. 1993., ed. *Distributed Cognitions. Psychological and Educational Considerations.* Cambridge: Cambridge University Press.

Sapir, E. 1971. *Language.* London: Rupert Hart Davis.

Schmuck, R., and P. Schmuck. 1992. *Group Processes in the Classroom.* 6th ed. Dubuque, Iowa: Wm. C. Brown.

Schön, D.A. 1983. *The Reflective Practitioner: How Professionals Think in Action.* New York: Basic Books.

Sharan, S. et al. 1984. *Cooperative Learning in the Classroom.* Hillsdale, N.J.: Erlbaum.

Sharan, S. ed. 1990. *Cooperative Learning: Theory and Research.* New York: Praeger.

Sharan, S., and A. Shaulov. 1990. Cooperative Learning, Motivation to Learn and Academic Achievement. In Sharan 1990.

Short, K.G., and K.M. Pierce, eds. 1990. *Talking About Books: Creating Literate Communities.* Hanover, N.H.: Heinemann Educational.

Shotter, John. 1993a. *Conversational Realities. Constructing Life Through Language.* London: Sage.

————. 1993b. *Cultural Politics of Everyday Life. Social Constructionism, Rhetoric and Knowing of the Third Kind.* Buckingham: Open University Press.

Sinclair, J. McH., and R.M. Coulthard. 1975. *Towards an Analysis of Discourse: The English Used by Teachers and Pupils.* London: Oxford University Press.

Slavin, R.E. 1990. *Cooperative Learning: Theory, Research and Practice.* Boston: Allyn and Bacon.

Smith, K.A., D.W. Johnson, and R.T. Johnson. 1981. "Can Conflict Be Constructive? Controversy Versus Concurrence Seeking in Learning Groups." Journal of Educational Psychology 73:651–663. Quoted by Slavin. 1990.

Stenhouse, L. 1975. *An Introduction to Curriculum Research and Development.* London: Heinemann.

Sutton, C. 1992. *Words, Science and Learning.* Buckingham: Open University Press.

Tann, S. 1981. Grouping and Group Work. In B. Simon, and J. Willcocks, eds. *Research and Practice in the Primary Classroom.* London: Routledge and Kegan Paul.

Tannen, Deborah. 1989. *Talking Voices. Repetition, Dialogue and Imagery in Conversational Discourse.* Cambridge: Cambridge University Press.

Thelen, H.A. 1960. *Education and the Human Quest.* New York: Harper.

Tizard, B., and M. Hughes. 1984. *Young Children Learning.* London: Fontana.

Todorov, Tzvetan. 1983. *Symbolism and Interpretation.* Translated by Catherine Porter. London: Routledge and Kegan Paul.

Von Dras, Joan Chandler. 1993. Empowerment Through Talk: Creating Democratic Communities. In Kathryn Mitchell Pierce and Carol J. Gilles, eds. *Cycles of Meaning.* Portsmouth, N.H.: Heinemann.

Vygotsky, Lev S. 1978. *Mind in Society. The Development of Higher Psychological Processes.* Cambridge: Harvard University Press.

———. 1981. The Instrumental Method in Psychology. In J. Wertsch, ed. *The Concept of Activity in Soviet Psychology.* New York: Sharpe.

———. 1992. *Thought and Language.* Revised and Edited by Alex Kozulin. Cambridge: The Massachusetts Institute of Technology Press.

Watson, J., and R.J. Potter. 1962. "An Analytical Unit for the Study of Interaction." *Human Relations* 15(3):245–263.

Webb, N. 1980. "An Analysis of Group Interaction and Mathematical Errors in Heterogeneous Ability Groups." *British Journal of Educational Psychology* 76(1):266–276.

———. 1982. "Group Composition, Group Interaction and Achievement in Cooperative Small Groups." *Journal of Educational Psychology* 74(4):475–484.

Wells, G. 1989. "Language in the Classroom: Literacy and Collaborative Talk." *Language and Education* 3(4):251–273.

Wells et al. 1990. Creating Classroom Communities of Literate Thinkers. In Sharan 1990.

Wertsch, James V. 1985. *Culture, Communication and Cognition: Vygotskian Perspectives.* New York: Cambridge University Press.

———. 1991. *Voices of the Mind. A Sociocultural Approach to Mediated Action.* London: Harvester Wheatsheaf.

Westbury, I. 1973. "Conventional Classrooms, Open Classrooms and the Technology of Teaching." *Journal of Curriculum Studies* 5(2):99–121.

Widdowson, H.G. 1978. *Teaching Language as Communication.* London: Oxford University Press.

Wilkinson, A.M. et al. 1965. *Spoken English. Educational Review* Occasional Publication No. 2. University of Birmingham School of Education.

Wilkinson, A., A. Davies, and D. Berrill. 1990. *Spoken English Illuminated.* Milton Keynes: Open University Press.

Wilson, M.J. 1976. *Pupils' Responses to Literature in Small Teacher-led and Pupil-led Groups: A Study of Pupils' Oral and Written Responses During the First Three Years of Secondary School.* Unpublished M.Sc. thesis, University of Lancaster.

Yager, S., D. Johnson, and R. Johnson. 1985. "Oral Discussion, Group to Individual Transfer, and Achievement in Cooperative Learning Groups." *Journal of Educational Psychology* 77(1):60–66.

Index